SEASONS OF MUSING

SEASONS OF MUSING

A Book Of Poems

Abiodun Alphonsus Ehindero

authorHOUSE®

AuthorHouse™
1663 Liberty Drive
Bloomington, IN 47403
www.authorhouse.com
Phone: 1-800-839-8640

Published by AuthorHouse   06/21/2013

ISBN: 978-1-4817-6467-4 (sc)
ISBN: 978-1-4817-6466-7 (e)

Library of Congress Control Number: 2013910948

CONTENTS

WAR and PEACE

NATURE COUNTRY LIFE AND SEASONS

LOVE AND PASSION

POLITICS

RELIGION AND SPIRITUALITY

DEDICATION

SEASONS OF MUSING is dedicated to all of you who were born and spent your early life in the rural towns and villages of the country. To those of you, with whom I share similar backgrounds, routines, thoughts and feelings.

Abiodun Ehindero
December 31st 2012

ACKNOWLEDGEMENT

My thanks go to you, friends in the poetry group of the Gather. Com community. Your encouragement and comments on my postings motivated me towards publishing this collection—SEASONS OF MUSING. Thank you my Jamaican friend Dennis Gilman; my countryman O. Akinwunmi and my Russian friend Svetlana Goryacheva.

Soli Deo Gloria.

LIFE & DEATH

CAROLINE I

In the bowel of mother earth,
In the land of the people of the rising sun
Far away she lays in her final rest,
Until that trumpet call.
Her name was Carol
So fresh and sweet
Like the Christmas Carols.
Graceful as the swan
And gentle as the lamb.
Like the nectar bird or the butterfly
Or the pollen harvesting honey bee
tenderly visiting the anthers;
She never hustled or gulped but gently sipped
From cupid's cup of juice
for just a short while.
Her tongue no single barb contained.
From her lips no words emerged profane.
And out from her heart the purest fragrance oozed.
No evil plans or acts covered with sweetest toast.
No trade mark twisting of me, round her little finger.
Just fine, soft velvety love from that heart
so tender, so kind.
Carol I still sing daily
The Carol.
Not at Christmas only.

THE RESPONSE OF THE DEAD

We file past in a show of last respect.
We file past our eyes drenched in tears.
Our hearts full of fear.
Tears
Meant for you and our trembling selves
Surely in equal shares.
Fears
Not for what awaits you there
For all imperfections here on earth
But the nearness, sureness, of our ends as well
Here on earth.

We walk with you this final stretch in measured steps
To the gate of your new abode,
Back with mother earth
From where you did sprout
and to which you now return.
The soil
Whose fruits you reaped in toils
To feed and grow
Now asked that you be sowed,
To hand back what she had loaned.

We walk now,
Unlike you, with our crowns to God
Our faces to this distracting world
And hence are blind
To the bright celestial light and signs.
The many thousand rehearsal nights
A dozen or more of such special heats
Along this dreary stretch
Have left our blindfolds still in place.

"Then watch my eyes as you progress
Read my lips and reap the message
Let me transmit to you through these eyes
And lips of the dead,
That light, the message from the skies.
That light you cannot see and the message
you cannot hear
Since you walk the world
Your eyes and ears away from the Sky,
Your hearts glued to the detracting world
The blindfolds still in place.
I move now unlike you on my back
With eyes and heart towards the clouds
My humbled heart, in silent talk with God.
And so read me now and clearly too.
Read me friends before that gate
Reap all you can your ways to mend
And drop the blindfolds as you leave
Goodbye."

MY HOME CHAPEL

For sure I know that I must die
"For dust thou art
And to dust must thou return"
Just when and how I do not know
But then I know for sure that when I die
That bell over there must surely toll
And then a niche of mission land
Be mine for ever to hold.
Except I am lost at sea or burnt and ashes lost
Which I pray for me will not be His choice.
Then this chapel I ask
that I be kept to recline
For just a short while,
For all that want to sight or snare
To file past my mocking stare.
Chapel of Resurrection, the courage fount.
My last abode above the ground
And then the six feet room below.
Our fortress here you are, we know.
To evil storm, let not this home succumb
Like that mountain rock there behind those trees
So their love and faith should be.

FRIENDS TILL THE END

When the stuff for mugs and glasses dry off or dwindle
And crowds of jollying friends reduce to singles.
When the bell rings not at the door or clang at the gate
And all you hear is a distant hail.
Worry not, for the crowd will surely return again
For the feast;
at your burial party.
Their remaining gain.

STILL BATTING AT NINETY EIGHT

Raised on herbs, barks and roots
Whose throat was never a route
For the white man's drugs until long past his noon
Knowing only the needle with a thread as tail;
Still stood firm but just a little frail
at the time post of ninety eight.
Daily, he walked gingerly to the Altar for his holy meals.
But since he hit his century,
The strength in his limbs slowly vacates.
His eyes not all objects do finely locate
He swings and blocks with many faults
And I know soonest, he will be caught,
bowled out; or *Leg—before—wicket.*
Swing not old man; keep steady.
Keep blocking, the next two overs.
And of course the inning would be over.
God willing.

CHILD VICTIM

Goodbye
Village hunting fields.
Goodbye
Fine sand of the village wrestling grounds.
Goodbye soccer.
Goodbye sports.
Welcome, pain and misery.
Welcome, years of adult gloom
Gift of the thunder from the ground.

Fair lady,
Princess of Wales;
Can you melt these stony hearts
Straighten these crooked minds
And ban these horrid mines
That ruin such life as mine?
Tell me, my lady.

Note:
This poem was written a mere one week before the death of princess Diana, after watching a documentary on her visit to a community in a mine clearing area in an African country, probably Angola.

BACK IN GEAR

When in those youthful vibrant days
Heaven sent its rain and shine
Without the weakest request of mine
I worked, cared, and shared
Enjoyed the warmth and gifts of life.
And kept the peace with friends and all.
For some I tilled; and others I planted.
Others still, I watered and weeded.
But for self, not enough hay was made
for the rainy day.
For when those hairs would grey,
The limbs grow weak; and nerves fray.
These regret filled days are daily made
more painful by people's corrosives words sprayed
For the selfless service they termed some foolish acts
But Heaven's sweet consoling whispers and calls
Lift up my troubled spirit.
Putting my gaze, hope and trust, back in gear.

UNTILL WE MEET AGAIN

Opposite a freshly done heap
With pale drying flower wreaths
Lies her place—her new abode,
just six feet or so
In the belly of the hard rocky terrain.
Between an older heap
And this new dug-out in the bowel of mother Earth
stands a dead tree.
Not a huge tree
But that of average girth,
Strongly rooted, hard to the core,
Creamy white; but dead.

Dead.
Roots unexposed; undestroyed.
Trunk, branches, unhacked; unburnt.
Standing firmly, but dead.
Dead,
In this rural grave yard; the last earthly abode
Of our beloved *Abiodun*.
But why?
Why is your grave Cecilia, at the very foot
Of this tree that died at its prime,
Like you at fifty-two?

The glare is strong and the wind still.
No birds fly as I scan the sky
And none is singing too!
Perhaps in sorrowful contemplation
They retired to the trees.
The trees, the palms, the reeds
stand motionless like this dead tree.
Like you in there, listening to the parting Psalm
Incensing your entry.

I look around the mourning lot
To see the faces that you loved
And those for whom you really cared;
Sad and swollen.
Eyes reddened, by days of running tears.
I see the white mourning dresses of your children
Appear dull and brown in sympathy
With this surrounding gloom.
Not even these Frangipani trees
in late season bloom;
Their fallen petals strewn on these older graves around
Would lift the gloom
Of this bereaved group as
the fluid of sorrow flow freely
Rising from the steaming hearts;
Spilling onto the dugout soil of Cecilia's grave;
Since her new neighbour the dead tree
Has no petals to shower.

Surely;
Like this tree standing here
In the valley of this majestic rock,
Strong and firm in death;
You are now perhaps standing there in heaven
With your Guardian Angel
Before Him, the Lord;
The Rock of Ages.
Biodun, Cecilia,
"Take not the millipede for food.
Eat not the earthworm there
There in glorious heaven please.
But whatever food is served.
Served to the dead who live
The souls triumphant.
Eat"
Requiescat in pace
Amen.

THE SAND GLASS

Three faulty counts
And the grains flow down.
Now; only by divine act
Can some fusion form
Among these fine selected grains,
To clog the straight and stop this drain
halfway gone.
Only by His wish.

LOST IN THOUGHT AT FATHER'S SIDE

These arms to which the virgin forests succumbed
And were transformed, to hectares of thriving tree crops.
These arms that did the swampy Fadama convert
To mammoth heaps of early yams farms.
The arms that made twenty thousand much smaller heaps
On savanna lands
every year.
These arms and legs that swam the great rivers at flood,
Laying bamboo and sticks, in rickety bridge constructions
Now hang sagging, wrinkled and lean.
The muscles and shoulders; strong powerful seats
Of the biting poles of the District and Resident officers' palanquin;
Deny completely the glorious conquests of years past.
His frame; that was once the magnet
That attracted and indeed charmed the sharers of his heart
Some who subsequently owned rooms under his roof
Appears truly ancient and in transit.
What remain unconsumed;
Not wrecked by time and the storms of life are
his memory; his warm inviting smiles
His noble and loving heart.

A STEALTHY COWARD

Stealthily but surely
He makes his rounds.
He could come unheralded
the next second,
Or some few seconds away.
The next minute,
Or some minutes away.
The next hour,
Some hours.
The next day
In the next few days.
He could come the next week,
Or just some few weeks to come
One month
Few months.
In the coming year
A few years grace
Yes he could come in normal strides
Snail slow or
In a flash!
But surely he will come
Like the distant dawn
And then the morning sun.
Executioner!
I know you are around,
For you drug me a little every night.
And so, the surprise is lost
You come when you choose
For that final, refreshing sleep
Come stealthy coward.

MY DESIRED LAST ROOM

Not for me a concrete grave
With marble slabs,
My naked ribs and limbs and
A frightening grinning skull to store.
Not for me I firmly insist
A casket of plated metal or shining steel
Or that made of some treated wood
That the sharp claws of rot and roots
And the crushing bites of termites resist.
Not for me the grave head marble stone
A jumbled heap of glass wreath
A structure that mimics a home
And an epitaph which from the barest truth departs.

Give me that grave
Which after a season's rains
Cause my soil blanket to collapse
asking for a re-fill.
Then plant an evergreen
A fichus or the like
At the head of the grave
To draw nourishment from my brain
My heart arteries and veins.
Then on me now the evergreen,
Hang a plastic tag with my names
and dates engraved.
A little replaceable wooden cross
To announce the faith I lived.

THE MUD–BRICK PIT

Out of the mud-brick pit
Came the limb bones and skull
Of a man many years buried.
The skull,
With a frightening mocking grin
Starring penetratingly through
fist size sockets as if in
cruel satisfaction saying
"My friend,
This pit a mirror represents.
What you see is you unfrocked
Some lonely bones some days to come.
All labour lost
All love and treasure gone!
And you, mere bones
In the womb of mother earth remain"

TIME AND MAN

In the fortieth hour,
It was sleep, food and stare.
The fortieth day,
The world was all cares.
The fortieth month,
Thrill play and tears.
The fortieth year,
Love, hate and fears.

THE CORPSE

That calm; that peace on his face
As he laid in state,
Denied the rot beneath gearing.
Which in a few hours will swell and implode
In the quiet of his new abode,
Down there in the womb of mother earth.
A messy end to one existence;
A corrupt start to life without end.
But then, as seeds, we surely must rot to germinate
To transform to the new life.

THE DEAD TREE

Great tree
You stand majestic
in this surrounding green.
Indifferent to the storms
At peace with the scorching sun.
Your trunk;
Charred by seasons of fire
Have left your heart unburnt.
I see the wood peckers come and go
Sounding your health in ringing tones.
The others too;
Great grand offspring of those
that courted your bosom then;
Perch to commune.
On those stout, creamy white, skeletal limbs.
What path in life
What foods; what cures
What supplications
What attributes of life
Have kept you now alive in death?
You are alive
More alive than the living.
Show me a glimpse of your green
Lend me a leaf to cover my span
To live my death like you in splendour
Among the living
Among the dead but living.

VICIOUS HUNT

Go; search the land!
Search the plains and
Burn down the slopes.
Roam the valleys
Search the caves
And the rock surfaces too for foot prints.
Call in the dogs to sniff the air
And flush the under growths.
Scan the canopies
And stealthily infiltrate the forest deep
Searching.
Search in the day and at night too!
Ask the ferns and the grasses of the path
Where he is
That robbed them of their dews.
Ask the winds
What they saw on their various routes
East to West;
North to South.
Search the groves and the swamps!
But do not be drawn by the roving devil's light
Into the bowel of the earth.
Search
Search for pressures in the sand
But watch out for traps of quick sand.
Search deep the snow covered land
But surely before new falls.
And if you fail in this great hunt
To find him that you want;
Come back home with booby traps laid
On every turn of the trail.
And if you loose
Find a way to sweep clean
Things that are his
That he be no more
What you could not be.

THE HEAD SPRINGS

From sweat and blood; from troubled hearts,
Ooze vibrant or soulful lines to the Muse's delight.
Mourners lengthy emotional appraisal lyrics
Unrehearsed; moving and tears provoking
but poetically delicious.
Lines enjoyed by ears sorrow unaffected
From a distance listening.

Sing the song O Israel, of your losses and woes.
Sing in the land of the Nile, reign of the wicked Pharaoh.
Sing the song of your long exile in Babylon
The song too; dear blacks of the Southern cotton fields.
Your songs,
That loathe, sweat, longing, and whips provoked.
Ethereal
Power filled
Heart lifting spirituals now old,
Still spirit spicing; like the Christmas Carols

Have you heard their songs?
Brief lines of the dispirited work gangs
Of the prisons and forced labour camps.
The rhymes
The rhythm
The reasons
The pains,
Oozing.

Great lines from the frontlines came bravely limping.
Reasons and deepest thoughts provoking.
Balaclava!
The charge of the Light Brigade!
"Half a league half a league
Half a league onward
All in the valley of death
Rode the six hundred"

O Flanders field!
O lines from Somme!
Flanders field where roots of poppies
In gallant veins did drink.
". . . the poppies grow
Between the crosses row and row
That mark our place and in the sky
The lark still bravely fly . . . ."
Death, suffering, pain and sweat
The head springs of lines eternal.

RESISTANCE

No, not now.
Not now for I have died
On my numerous trips.
Referred as it were to reseat this life's examinations
Innumerable times in my childhood.
And so not now; not now!
I shall not die!

The prints rejected the announcement
At thirty-four; at thirty-nine.
Again at forty-nine
Most common pruning stretch.
And now at sixty, I reject
The announcements once again
"With deepest regret . . . ."
"In cherished, affectionate evergreen memory . . . ."
And so you, 'ill have to wait.
Wait 'till my 'teens are over the hills of youth
To read from the pages of the day
Their gratitude to God
"For a life well spent"

THE GRAVE YARD

Rows and rows of grey weather beaten
crumbling wooden crosses
Mark many heaps overgrown with weeds
Or occasionally barren, edged with stones.
Here and there, distinction even in death.
Sculptures of different makes and forms
Burst of concrete, metal or stone
Show above the leveling depth
In this sad, vast farm land of death.
There on one row, some fresh heaps
With seeds ripe or perhaps unripe
Reaped and re-planted.
Whose sprouting like others await
The trumpet sound of that fateful day.
Over there,
My choice of grave.
A lonely barren heap
Out of line with the rest
Flattered low after seasons of rain.
Unmarked.
Noted only in the pierced hearts
Of those he left behind.

THE PARROT, THE MUSE AND I

O Parrot of the graveyard forest fringe
I have on numerous sad trips
To this loudly silent garden of the dead
Amidst soulful mourning, prayer and songs
Heard your apparently unsympathetic chattering
As if commenting care freely on our sad proceedings.
Perhaps on what we failed to see or hear
Like what goes on in the minds of those gathered here.
The bereaved
Some, disheveled;
Others gazing emptily; lost, gone!
Those whose other halves they've come to return
To mother Earth

In your long habitation of this nearby forest
You have many grave side theatric witnessed
And surely some common thoughts of women truly dejected,
or seemingly affected, you have harvested
since human minds with great ease you do access.
But your chattering we cannot decode.
The thoughts to the Muse therefore I plead you release
The Muse, our common friend, whose mind language
I speak.

Here then are the thoughts from subsequent visits
Released by my avian associate
through the Muse our dear comrade.
The prevailing thoughts that some women harbour
At the demise of their poor mates.

"O death
Too stony bowelled; too blind to see
The fusion of my life, my heart to his;
Has drawn the scalpel through our mid
Splitting these Siamese twins
And killing both!
He, to rot in the bowel of the earth,
I, to wait and rot in this hell.
O death! Let me please to him now depart"

"Let my tears roll down for all to see
That I be cleared of the leprous tag—a witch!
But what you sow you sure must reap; the wise say.
So let those others that shared your flirting heart
Roll down tears for you in buckets full.
For I have shed mine too many times in cups full.
Now the contentious bone as they say,
a strange dog has snatched away.
But then, I shall not fail to pay you back
That, which I owe.
A quarter spade of earth dumped down on you
The last cascade of tears, just a ruse
And of course, a feigned slump!"

"The Lord is good; my God is great.
The One who gives and at will takes
There in your bosom I pray he stays
May your mercy with me abide as well
So, to new verdant pasture lead.

That I will not austere seasons in future meet
But perhaps at worst, just a little miss
The great times we have had.
It is well!
It is well!"

Oh, disabling helplessness; the child of true affection.
Oh, unsheathed callousness a tool for self-destruction.
True selfishness in spiritual language vested.
Dear muse, what says you as a perfect feeling
Of a woman in such or similar loss, seething?

"O human; there is no perfect feeling
Of a kind pure and good,
But an amalgam of a review
of yesterday, today, and tomorrow.
Which when goodness and love dominates,
Approaches the perfect feeling."

THE MOURNERS

A few days ago and
He would have passed unwept.
A curse!
For who dares to drum or cry
And ruin the peace of *Oluwo*
The god of our land.
Oro
A time when wailing wears the cloak
of muffled sounds.
With hands clasped on breasts
Higher up on the head,
Or thrown back with fingers meshed
behind the neck!
A time when the sockets of sorrow
Send their warm sweet torrents back
the other way down into
The depth of the heart;
Raising it to boil unseen.

But now a change in time
A time for the best in the art or act
To exhibit their gifts of voice and lyrics
Providing competing accounts of the life
of the deceased,
With minimum tears!
"Have you been there?"
"O yes I have dropped my share of tears.
So many women there
But *Aina* was as good as ever.
For I could see others stop to listen;
To copy!
And she was not lacking in tears too!"
"Will you go Joan?"
"Not now
Surely, not now.
Not with my stomach empty
I shall eat first for strength
To hit some good lyrics
Coupled with a good cry."

FROM SLEEP TO ETERNITY

That day he was not at the morning Mass
And so to me the senior truant
our mother came to ask.
I moaned a drowsy "morning ma"
Rolled, stretched and put my sleep back in gear.
Then came the sound of urgent knocking
That followed some unanswered calls.
The knocking grew to banging
The banging grew with more anxious voices
As they forced open a window of his room
Since the entrance door was locked; secured from within.
And there he laid; cold and stiff!
A visit in the night by the cruel thief
My 'good night' parting wish to him
Was unacceptable to the Lord.

TIME-2

Why reduce the seconds in your minute
Why shorten the minutes in the hour.
Why give the day new plumage to fly
quickly away to the land of yesterday.
Why rush so fast the gentle moon,
And make us sing the Carol so soon.
Time
How dare you rush me forward this fast
To meet your callous friend death
Who devours all encountered but you?
At double-trot you raced me all through
To this sixty-fifth post unrested; un-refreshed.
Whereas my old man is at his ninety nineth
And prays you step up his space for the home run.
Mine, I pray you slow down to a crawl.
But Time; when has prayers melted your stony heart?
Never.

NO BARRIERS

What can stop the down flight
Of those detached golden yellow and brown Autumn leaves
That the wind in passing dislodged
Or the breeze in whispers urged?
What can stop the snow, the flakes falling
Once they escape the tilted trays
Of the winnowers in the sky?
Who can stop the star shooting across the sky
When an Angel cuts it loose
From its titter in the galaxy?
What can stop the trip of the glorious sun
From East to West and not return
Under cover of night to the East; its home.
Its home, for the following morning trip?
Who can cause the million silvery threads of rain
To curve back, upwards;
Back to source
The ground, not to caress and bath again?
What can stop the great plunge of Victoria's
massive sheet of water at the lip of the fall
From hitting the huge trough below?
What can stop these hairs greying
These eyes failing
These muscles sagging
This gait wobbling
This sixty five years magnificent pump weakening
And slowing down to a final stop
Someday soon?
Nothing
Nobody

CAROLINE II

Sleep on dear Carol in your Oriental bed
In the womb of a pacific land;
A piece by death you owned these many years past
Their tremors and quakes may shake and crash
Their tsunamis and typhoons may flood in rage
But none can my beauty stir to wake.
Not even loves more potent whispers and thoughts
Can your heart in that peace conjure back to life.

From your life rare sweet fragrance oozed
As from a garden of the evening primrose.
Carol, soon will my allotment be dug too,
And back to soil I shall come.
And then we meet at the trumpet call,
When you shall rise from the land of the rising sun;
And I from that of the tropical sun
To meet Him; the Risen Son.
Until that call my dear,
Requiescat in peace.
Amen.

ETERNITY

The good works that you do, for sure, after you, do live.
But spans of life of theirs they too have
Since they, in the blood and memories of generations thrive
Their sizes dwindling;
Colours and out-line fading with time
Until forgotten.

Your wealth and all that you leave behind
Varying spans, time likewise grants.
For they, like furrow in the desert
The wind soonest fills with sand.
Like sand castles on the beach braving sea tides
Collapsing in time to continuous assault
Like the morning mist that blocks Phoebus' vision,
But with time is licked by his smiles.

If heaven's will, all seasons you strive to do.
Your neigbour as yourself to love you choose.
His faults your forgiving heart truely expels,
Just as many times as the air you do exhale;
Then Heaven's eternity for you is safe.
But on Earth eternity does exist!
As Calliope; Erato with others insist
That if in closeness their breath you inhale
Their wise thoughts on your mind imprint.
And if these, in lines and verses you with faith bequeath,
Then your name and labour forever will live.
So a double eternity here and yonder, to poets avail.
If his heart is routinely on the trail.

NIGHTLY REVIEWS

In the days of targets setting.
Of multiple goals challenging.
Days of adrenal flow, long and sizzling,
When these limbs; this body daily took some beating.
Sending me wobbling into the waiting embrace
Of death's lovelier, kinder comrade sleep
I spent the nights recouping.
But now with all goals nearly accomplished
And adrenal flow and other agents to base line ebbed,
No deep slumbers are required to recoup
But time in the night my yesterdays to review.
Ruminating on times and actions of years past
Of rain sustaining clouds the wind drifted away
Of harvested crops Phoebus smiles denied to dry
Of glittering fleet footed mirages
on various routes of my search trips.
Of fish caught and lost, slipping from my grip,
since held by the mid or tail.
Of hay unmade in Phoebus happy moods
Of seeds of my stock now fruiting.
Of friends and mates many departed and
Myself like a child uncollected at close of school
All alone in the yard; afraid, dejected.
Of trials and pains unconverted to heavenly treasure.
Of the society and country adrift, rudderless; anchorless.
Of my eventual journey home.

END OF SUMMER

The warmth recedes like a descending flag
in a controlled glide,
Down the staff
As the sun frowns and weakly smiles a dozen times
in the hour.
A habit that worsens with the approaching sound
of winter's steps hurrying.
As autumn, the forerunner prepares the way,
Browning, yellowing, and pinking.
Splashing gold in different shades.
Then disrobing all for a naked parade
In readiness for months of nude slumber.
It dawned on me and I shuddered
That I, in autumn of life now exist, and soon
With this ample splash of sliver on my crown
And the wilting of the skin; will like these leaves
the glide to earth and decay undertake.
Living my winter in the soil
Springing at the trumpet call.
To blossom
And flourish in heavenly summer.

THE WEEPING CHILD

What ails you my little girl?
That you so loudly cry?
Who ruffled those elegant peace wings?
Of your free unburdened mind
Tipping over the lachrymal glands
In those lovely, Angelic eyes.
Is it the cockroach there that on its back lies?
Or that big buzzing intruding hunter's fly?
Was your piece of meat snatched by that thief?
That dog over there lying on the leather cushion riff?
Or perhaps some biting reminder from that pinching begger
the Oliver Twist locked up in your stomach?
Though your tears no longer cascading flow
But just lazily roll, halt, then roll
Down the pair of salt tracks
Your peace in truth is not really back.
What my girl, can your peace restore?
Will a sweet lullaby that peace conjure?
Or just a piece of cake and a mother's hug?

THE PORCUPINE

Some days ago you were alive
Proudly alive
A mobile battery of deadly missiles
Untouchable even to the kings and
princes of the kingdom.
What then could have laid you low
this early noon of your life?
Was death itself unscarred to
confront such a formidable foe?
Has death no respect for such like you
a wearer of death?
Or unknown to you,
your Achilles' heel betrayed by a friend?
Perhaps.
Perhaps.

RENEGED

You gave me hope.
That hope,
Like a precious glass globe
handled not with great care
Dropped on a stone floor bare,
and into smithereens shattered.
The fragments,
Like shrapnel scattered.
Projectiles flew upwards,
Puncturing my hitherto joy inflated heart
Now in painful bleeding.

A FRIEND PASSES AWAY

Receding watery glitter of a desert route
Fast fading brightness of the shooting star
No wind, no storm, no rumblings betrayed his flight
A feather touch tipping of a seemingly firm existence
Re-affirming the nothingness of our most treasured possession
And the greatness of that Power that is.

A PARTING PLEA

Do not at my grave side fake a faint
The in-thing most people claim.
Or, into my pit a fall to feign.
To be held back by some unconvinced arms
As the mourners end the soil scooping rounds.
For such theatricals no love nor loss confirm
But meant only for the watching eyes
Who want to see the proof of love in styles
But know for sure the strands are fake
And still approve with brief nose blowing sobs.
Squeezing some wretched drops
for the wiper to spread and mop
As the crowd slowly disperses.

I bid you to hold your frame erect and firm
And let the tears cascade down your sorrow contoured face
To wash away the era of my reign.
Give no chance for my ghost to hunt your life
But let your young heart; which too young to starve
fallow,
Just for a while ; a short while.
Then grow a new plant on the compost of our life together.
And from up there beyond the stars I,
with heavy celestial dew, the plant shall water.
That it may take and richly blossom.

ABIKU

Thrice I have come
Thrice I have gone
And thrice I shall come and go again
If what I want you do not give.
Your hoe, you have hidden
Your garbage dump-site you claim is full
And the bush you claim will reject my corpse
But be careful woman
For when I want I go, and go I will
If what I want you do not give.
You brand my thigh with hot metal rod.
My face your blade loves the best.
But hinder me?
They will never
For these awards make me great
Among my people from where I come.

Now with your plea I will stay
Yes I will stay.
But what I want I must have.
Seven black hens; seven white pigeons.
Seven rolls of white thread; seven black ones.
Seven pepper fruits wrapped in leaves.
A pot, and a cooking spoon.
All wrapped in a white cloth
And thrown into the seventh river at flood
On the seventh day of my re-birth.
To keep my seven wives occupied
For the seventy-seven year I agreed to stay
If not, I shall go.

MY MOODS AND THE MUSE

Whenever my health on rough and stormy water sails
When this body is lashed by strong waves of stress and pain
Erato the Muse into my sorrow filled heart glides
Inspiring, soothing, transmitting her love filled lines.
Transforming the mood
Like the soft tranquil moon
The night's darkness dispersing.
And I write.

At times when bugs of worries my system invade
Heating the blood to forbidden range
To the chants of Gregory I turn in haste.
After hours of throat filled, hearty chanting
Behold the retreat down the rugged slope
To the range, the level of easy flow,
Filling my heart with joy and hope.

When the clouds of guilt and fear
From crimes of thought, words and deeds
my heart envelope.
Then after a penance clean and clear restores my peace, joy
and hope,
The Muse takes over; letting my mind flow with lines spiritual
And I write.

TO POET R.E.G. ARMATTO

Dear Armatto
I have read your piece
On how you wanted to go
And so hope
That through some celestial 'scope
Or power unknown to me
You can see this piece of mine.

I would have wished you loved to go
In your "lovely" way but alone
In the crash and blaze.
Like those consumed by imperial craze,
In those horrible pacific kamikaze dives.
I would have wished you spared a thought
For those with you who never wished
For mangled limbs or charred remains
But bones unfleshed and white in coffins deep.

But since you got the second best
On land and not in air
A tangled mass, a mangled mess
No "shining brightness for my last embrace"
Will you repeat your wish when next you come?
As for me, I want to go
If you must know
When all my grains are brown
and harvest birds sing their songs of joy.
I want to go bent double on my rounds
With a stick in front a meter away.
A heart-warming timbre in my box.
And when it comes, the priest
With Host, Crucifix and balm;
A ring of them summoned from afar
Who love to see and receive my benediction
And sing the Te Deum to the Trinity.
To pull my lids and lips to close
To plug with wool, bathe and clothe
And planted back to where I grew.

SLEEP IS REST OR DEATH

Sleep
You are rest in the daily rehearsals,
Day or night
And *death* you are
When your reversal, for ever is lost.
The two sides of a coin you are for sure;
Head and tail; that's it.
Flip the coin, and one never knows
which in his way will fall.
I do not begrudge you death
When and how the final event of life you direct
Since this you keep to your chest.
So much have I enjoyed your kind restorations and peace, *sleep*
These twenty-four thousand nights and, scores of afternoons
That the coin, flipped, and turned head repeatedly, on landing.
And so I care not what you do to me, when you land tail
on the final day
When your name to death you change.
Not even if you decide in your callous manner
To haul me into a shark infested water
Roast me in hotest fire
Send me flying in the greatest twister
Or entomb me in the arctic snow.
No bitterness will I show;
Since eternal rest follows yonder.

THE SNAIL'S PATH ON THE WALL

Despite this pack,
your problem back.
And the uphill task
of the long route.
You made your way
Sowly, up and across
this world of walls.
You made this path
Your silvery route of conquest
Of your Kilimanjaro, your Everest
Some pointer and beacons for us, who are enroute
Our personal Everest.

ABUJA DERAILED–1997 AD

Abuja!
No, Suleja!
Great city of the pottery queen.
What did the oracle say then?
What sacrifices did you offer to your ancestors
and the gods?
Before you were "born again"?.
Before your name change?
The name you so willingly surrendered
Perhaps for love of country
Now wears the garb of decadence and avarice
A city still being created; adorned in royal ornaments
Is grey, wrinckle, and senile.

Oh Suleja!
Did you fore-see this disaster
in their Abuja?
Did you surrender your glorious name
For a monster such as this creation?
Surely there must have occurred a mutation
at conception
In her genes for orderliness and decency.
Or perhaps a cancerous invasion
Of the desires, plans, goals and vision
Of the founding fathers, of Abuja.

Abuja
A city now drained of true cosmopolitan vibrancy
Where Grace and Beauty in their youth
got murdered,
Where Law and Order from the thrones
got banished.
And in their places
Filth, corruption, and disorder enthroned.

AT FORTY

I have done the stretch
That pruning distance
The last ten posts to the fiftieth year.
I have crossed the infested stream
Crossed before the flood that swept the bridge
The nocturnal *okete* passed,
Then came the light of day!
And so, towards the journey's end
I trudge.

THE DISCOUNTED YEARS

Life, it is said, begins at forty
And so the thirty-nine initial years
Are but preamble to life and so
Stand discounted.
As the biblical limit stands at three scores plus ten
I crave for just that then.

Now discount the thirty-nine
And my age is twenty five!
So, *Deo volente;*
I have forty-five good years unfretted!
Look not then for that advertisement
"With gratitude to God for a life well spent"
And the declaration of free food, free drinks
Soonest.

NEAR DEATH

My bellows have worked the furnace of life
these past sixty years
Without faltering.
Until this night of great fear
When I choked and gasped for breath
Jerked up from a deep slumber.
I choked.
Choked
For many seconds that the hour's apparel wore
I gasped for breath and thought I was gone!
O how unbelievably narrow, this lane
Separating here and yonder
How like the bubble at the end of the spittle thread
Hangs this dear life.

CHILD OF YOUR OLD AGE

For a clone of the human being
Look not to the country of Her majesty the Queen.
Or to the land of the Statue of Liberty
"God's own country"
For here before you is a clone of you
In body and thought
In speech and all
You are the same.
O boy!
Those things in you that I adore
As well as others that I abhor
Are all there in this "clone" of yours.
Lord; how I pray his other half—his wife
Will grow the patience that I have
For that flip side of your smiles
That precipitates in me, intense frowns and at times
Cascading tears.

ABUJA RESURRECTS—2005 AD

O El-Shaddai
Maker of heaven and earth
Father of the risen Christ
Creator of our El-Rufai,
This city's ministering Angel.
Who stood not at the tomb's entrance
Like that Angel, to announce His resurrection
And give to the women, direction
But sits at his office desk, away from the city's entrance
And gives instructions
Rare in this society so corrupt; so fake
Resurrecting a city long decayed.
We thank you El-Shaddai and pray
That for a while you let this Angel stay
And not withdraw him to heaven his home,
For Abuja's new life and glow
A deeper taproot and fresh laterals to grow
And the progress Rubicon cross.

THE CHAMELEON AND THE LIZARD

We walk the earth so gingerly
For fear of creating punctures.
We change our coat colours in sympathy
With shades surroundings
The leaves when green
The grass when brown
The grey rocks and the dark red soil
The black sooth of the burnt bush
And the greyish brown of the dead leaves
of the forest floor.
We change for all along our routes
But yet man dislikes our cautious ways
Their medicine men rewarding us with a slow painful death
Clamped and tied limbs and tail
In the grip of some sticks
And left in the sun to die;
Then charred with herbs in their
Medicine charring pots.

We rustle the undergrowth
The dried up leaves of the forest floor
And wake up humans in their sleep.
We race on their mud-wall homes and
Hide at play in the numerous cracks!
We jump on them, disrupting their works
And ford their drinking water ponds.
Yet little is done to us
For our ways and unchanging colours they know,
But yours are cloaked in mystery
The slow, gingerly taken strides and ever changing colours
The bulging, suspiciously rolling eyes and sticky darting tongue
That renders fatal kisses to unsuspecting preys
All these, men cannot bear.
And so you lose for efforts to be fair.

REMINDER TO MY CHILDREN

My life in the countryside
Has glued my heart to the greens.
To the flowers of the fields
The fascinating trunks and canopies of great trees
The slopes, and the rolling hills.
But my life at the quarries,
The tanks of slurry
And the heat of cement kilns
Has my spirit averse to concrete
And so, no grave and slabs of concrete
Nor walls and forms of sandcrete
But a pit of naked soil my sides to grip.
No metal casket the bones to store
Just a humble, simple wooden box.
No disgusting multi coloured glass wreaths
But bunches from gardens fresh.
Plant some annuals on my heap
And then a ficus for a head tree

Bury not your dead when freshly dead
Lest it be rejected for hurrying home.
Store in morgue for months unending
And run around to raise some loans
To mark your loss in food and wine.
It gets coffin or grave sore
For lying too long
On just its back these many years.
So starve the home and raise fresh loans
To ease its pain in a true child's way.
Though he be burning brightly in hell.

Buy admission placement for your child
Or an impersonator hire to write his tests
And claim the brilliance that isn't his.
Pay the teacher for fake scores and grades
Or source the fund for leaked question sets
or 'expo' the trade name!
Thus contribute your inglorious lot
To the decay and destruction of our state.
Make scripts marking your seasonal harvest time
For milking seekers of unmerited grades.
Make that innocent young lady fail
Despite her brilliance and her scores
For refusing stripping and fondling behind your door,
While the boys pay you in cash and goods.
Make the girls pay *kia-kia pronto!*
By shameless visits to their sacred valley grottos.
Your rewards should not stack up in heaven in sets,
But must be taken here on earth,
As and when encountered.

Tell your friend to wait here awhile
And while you detour he waits in vain
Invite across a booby trap trench
A load of spikes and thorns to catch the fall.
Then stab him fast deep and sure
That he mightn't turn for Caesar's words
And then acquire all that you jointly own.

TRULY THE WEALTHIEST EVER

Come down back to earth Onassis
Come back Rocky
Come down here Donald Trump
Come; open the gate Bill Gate
Come down too Roman Abramovich
Lord of the Virgins Richard Bronson, come.
And you too Steve Jobs of Apple
Come all of you
To my place in the slum of Lagos
Send an Angel to represent
If no flight would come down to earth again
As it did on Easter Sunday.
Bring along your statements and balance sheets
With my notes to compare.
To choose on whom shall fall the nomenclature
The title of
The wealthiest man ever on planet earth

I dare say none of you will come an arm's length
of my exalted pedestal
When our individual wealth in Pound sterling,
Dollar, Franc or Yen exchange
to a common currency
"Health"!
Who amongst you men do match
Or when alive if dead, did match my wealth
Of fifty thousand seconds of road walk or trek per week?
Pump up your arm bands and request for
Your "pressure expenditures statesments"
And see if you have not criminally overdrawn
Above your honourable limit of one-twenty-eighty!
Unlike me a fine spender
Never in the red even at sixty-eight!
Health is wealth.

TORTUROUS LIVING

Three of the walls of my bedroom
A large window each proudly displays.
Each window a church or two confronts
But one, in addition, a mosque!
Except the little mosque with two loud speakers mounted,
all the churches deployed effectively four
To fight their war
With the "unborn again"; the infidels.

On days of great offensive—Sundays,
All fronts are alive all day.
With reluctance I exit my old fashioned
Cool prayers style church, a mile away
with the "Go in peace and serve the Lord"
To move back to my abode right at the warfront
To be pummeled in the preaching bombardments
with scores of alleluia shrapnel
And loads of "Praise God" debris
Falling in through the three wide ears of my room.
And when two or three in the encirclement
On the same unlucky night decide their vigils to hold
I am doomed!
"Good nights and sweet dreams" quickly degenerate
To raw nights, no dreams but anger and pain.

In alliance with these houses of prayer
The discordance of the neighbourhood motor parks
The senseless blaring by vehicles and bikes
on high ways and streets.
The clanging and banging from workshops on my street
The frequent all noon and all night partying on some streets
The cacophony from the terraced shops and markets
of this dense neighbourhood,
Put my nerves permanently on the edge,
My patience drained, my anger near always to
The boiling point.

THE CLASS OF 1962, MSMC ALIADE

There were in our second year some blossoming Atlas kids
And a few cousins or nephews of Tarzan too.
There was a small Lilliputian rank and in this
Little *Ochonu* found his peace.
Then the sickly and fragile limbed
With tears filled eyes ever ready to flood
Was where I truly belonged.
The mum's pet group; whose severed umbilical cords
Regenerated into apron strings and got severed again
By their departure to school far away from home
Was close to my group.

Later; a few swift footed Achilles emerged in the class
And one of them we thought, with consistency would rise
As a candidate perhaps, for the Nation's *Victor Ludorum*.
We had the English bug; and so played the cricket game.
The class did contribute a great breaker of bails and
Scatterer of stumps, to the school's first-eleven
Even as a junior!
That was little fragile me—Alphonsus.
There were those who with the parrot did compete
Then the Angels; and, the twisters of the sleeping dog's tail
O, there was John and there was Vincent the top whiz-kids!
And of course their worthy acolytes—
Our Archimedes and Einstein.
Our Newton, Cicero and the like.
There was too I must say, a cleric in the making
And of course he got the oil!
Climbed the ladder
Grabbed the mitre
And wait for it
The Bareta!!

I did not swim at the starters end shallow
Nor at the divers deep end did I wallow
But surely relished my commoners mid pool locus
Where with the invisible daughters of Zeus
I played and splashed and got in love
First with History's beautiful *Clio*
And then, with captivating *Calliope and Erato.*
For sure I did try great Caesar's tongue
But to the floor my tongue got tied
And I got sentenced to seat on the floor
Whenever my declensions went wrong,
My unseen translations refuse to conform.
But then, I sipped enough the *Laudate* to sing
The *Credo;* the *Gloria* and *Te Deum* to chant,
The school motto translate.
Quis ut Deus
Of course!
Who is like God?

TO RESTFUL SLEEP

When your rightly allotted slot
The mind, the brain in greed usurp,
All members of the body in sympathy revolt,
Resulting in your gliding return
As the mind and brain you dethrone.
And when you exit, and are truly gone,
All members are richly rewarded.

EPITAPH

These twin graves
With shared fence and gate
Contain the remains not of two hearts that did vows exchanged
Nor that of a set of lovely but unlucky twins
But siblings forty long months between
Who on the same night, the same death shared.
They were like flower's maturing buds
Yet unopened to the world
Its bees and other insects
Its birds and all
Who now, through death shared
As heavenly twin exist.

MIND MAIL

My loving old man
How immensely I miss you now.
Much more than I ever thought I would
When to a foreign land beyond easy trip I moved,
Thinking that my five and a half dozen years with you
Have moved me cleanly out of the range
Of a young child's attachment feelings.

The realisation of my immenent loss
As a result of your impending departure
Sinks in daily
Biting painfully
Like this winter chill blowing on me.
And I surely regret crossing the seas before your trip
But then, God's schedule I did not see
That before my return, your trip would be.

Faster than the lighting flash
My mind, across space do dash
Daily over hills and plains
And the deep wide roaring moat
Since to this land I came.
Then I see you thumbing the beads;
Or eyes gliding the walls of your room
Settling on each picture of your kids in turn
And some seeds from these too!
Sometimes I see you
Eyes fixed on the ceiling high
Or on the floor
Those brown and cream coloured tiles;
Heart and mind in review of times past
And in anticipation of your coming life.
That life after life.
Papa, can't you delay a little while?

Just a little while?
While these few knots I loosen
These huddles' cleared
These kernels just gathered shelled.
Then to you with metal wings, through the clouds I shall speed
Before your journey by your side to be.
Or at worst arrive when in the morgue
You have not slept for too long.

DEO GRATIAS

Your incessant plea
That your sojourn down here be ceased
Has at last His blessing received.
Thus ending your singular unebbing fear
Of seeds or their offsprings untimely returned to earth
While you stare.
Terminating too, that discomfort;
That loneliness you rightly felt and fought
Since all friends; age-groups, relations
And other peers have gone.
And down; down the ladder strungs
A required decent you made for new friends
New acquaintances
While waiting for this journey home.

BATSMAN CYRIL

"How-wiz-that!"
'Out'
Gone!
Through the dark, cold exit tunnel
Gone!
To the bright light at the end inviting
Drawn.

In that inning; you hit some elegant sixes
Piling up to the precious century
Despite waves of frontal assaults of varying depths; varying
strengths.
A vicious mobile encirclement
With ambush on every possible escape trail.

Then came their thunderous jubilant call
Of 'how-wiz-that!' as if unsure
Of the *leg-before-wicket* obvious to all.
But sure or not the cry did come.
Father dear.
Resquiescat in pace
Amen.

TITI AT TWELVE

The sprouting of those two chest knobs
That you with great excitement love
On discovery
And which to lovely boobs will transform
Unknown to you undeniable exhibits are,
For your upcoming popular "banishment and exile"
From your father's home
To a home hitherto unknown
For life!

MIRIAN MAKEBA IN THE URN

O dust in the precious urn
Ashes of the lady of songs
Remains of Mama Africa; sing!
Sing, songstress of freedom; sing!
Encore the last phatha phatha
Of Baia Verde
Sing Miriam that lovely parting number
To the world
Your own brand of "Till we meet again"
Sing as you step out of this hollow stage
This Urn
Into the loving embrace
of the sea
Kissing the smooth brows at rest
Clasping onto the massive rising chests
And the huge enveloping biceps
As they rise and fall repeatedly
In the joy of your final home coming.
Removed from the created artificial cold
Of the dreary morgue of Castel Vulturno.

Sing ashes of Miriam sing.
Sing, queen of the stage for tenants of the sea.
Sing again,
The click song, and Lakutshn, Ilanga
Malaika and Iya Guduza
Uthando Luyaphela and
Sindiza Nge cadillacs
Attracting fishes moving in great shoals;
Their hunters forgetting to prowl!

Sing for them, Kilimanjaro
Table Mountain
The naughty little flea
Sweet flowing Suliram

And Olilili.
And since the night has fallen; sing,
Night Must Fall!
These and all the elegant songs
That failed to soften and *click*
The stony bowels of those great-white sharks on land
Will in ashes dissolved, calm
The great-whites of the cape's water.
Making them with dolphins compete
Looping
Racing
Skipping with glee
Mixing with swimmers at the beach!
Harmless.
Harmless.
Miriam;
Ride now in deep currents across seven seas
To your coasts of choice.
Coasts of lands your songs did tour.
Ride in, with the morning tides
Or that, rolling in late at night
With tidings, yes,
Of One more dance.
Of great-whites of your land, now to dolphins changed.
Adieu *Mama Afrika.*

WAR & PEACE

RECOLLECTION

As the droning grew louder
With the planes getting nearer
All heads turned skywards; eyes scanning
Each pair hoping to be the first
To glimpse the metallic birds
of the white man passing.
We never did;
Since the planes flew high above the clouds
Perhaps on their way to the desert front
To the North.
Or to the forces at the Horn
To the East
Where the empire strengthened rulers of the waves
were slugging it out with
The swastika inspired pasta-pizza troops
Of Benito Mussolini
Perhaps.
Perhaps.

A LOOK-OUT CALLS TO ARMS

I am *Eleesu*
Have you heard my name?
Yes I am *Eleesu*
Your eyes at the base of the clouds
Your ears on the forest floor
The look-out, of the monkey colony.
I am where I am placed.
Have you heard me now?
Wake up! Wake up!
Wake up the right flank toughs
Wake up now, left flank troops
Wake up central fighting group.
Wake up; you men of the forest clan.
Are you asleep?
Bring their heads home, as you have always done
And pay homage to, the king our lord.
Bring in the heads to adorn the city wall
Stuck in the wall facing outwards
To scare invaders all.
Listen!
Their camp stirs!
The hooves move to the right.
Wake up! Wake up!
Blunt the push of the *Tapa* hordes.
They are moving fast to the right
Blunt the movement fast
I have warned.
So now, bring praise to this flute
Bring peace to these eyes deep in debt
And stop the hills sucking the throbs
Of my drumming chest.
Wake up!
Wake up!

THE PEP-SONG OF THE OLD WARRIOR'

Great warriors
What is in the bush
that you take to the paths?
Perhaps it is the spear grass
Perhaps some grass blades
Or the black tips of mere shafts approaching!
What scares you in battles?
What will cause an arrow in flight to retreat?
What startles the long smooth shafts?
What hurtles down from above,
That the ground cannot hug?
What chills the blood in your veins?
At worst you are maimed
Or then, you are missing!
And worst still, I say
You answer two names on the same day!
So, blow the horn; blow it hard.
Drive fear into the enemies' hearts
Stir the blood in our vessels, flowing fast
Scuttling fears out of your pounding chests.
Bring the flute to action fast
And let memories flow
Bringing back our heroic past.
Our forefathers deeds on the battle fields.

Did we not come in water and blood?
And who departs in blood but the brave.
Go then to where the shafts fly.
Pluck the suckling cubs of the lion in the lair
Pick the eggs from the guarded nest
Of the mountain eagle on the crest.
Swiftly

Go; snatch the kill from the feeding leopard's clutch
Swiftly
Uncoil the python from around its eggs
And pick them off before it lunges.
Follow where the smooth shafts go
And turn back home
Only when their heels in flight you see
And arms unattended lie discarded.

RETURN OF OUR CIVIL WAR COMBATANT

He came back a hero from the front
Of a war many years bitterly fought.
His side, the Federal troops, a clear victory won
But for peace among brothers, unceremoniously deflated
And re-christened—"No victor, no vanquished"
For the country's cohesion to stand.
Joe, a sergeant major in his camouflage
Proudly roamed the village streets
Every day to the admiration of tailing kids
He roamed and roamed till the day grew dark
Giving his uniform respite only late at night.

At the brew house or the palm wine drinking joints
His exploits at the various fronts he lavishly recalled.
O boy! What a great fighter our local lad was!
For he led his company, or detachment in the war.
Every thrust,
Fast and powerful their break-through was
Such that made the German blitzkrieg
but an ordinary Boer Great Trek.
As for our hero's invincibility; well, well,
That secret we will never know
Since no amount of booze
Would our hero's secret succumb.

BY FIRE; NOT FLOOD WATER

Now, no mail or other metal armour
But special vests of materials light
Piercing projectiles to calmly thwart.
Now, no arrows, spears and javelin throwing strongmen
Behind shield-carrying sword-wielding hack men
But bullet spraying; grenade lobbing storm troops
With spicing of tube-lunched and other system missile groups.

Now, no fire—and—reload balls and powder guns
But howitzers, mortars and self-propels with shell mussels
fed in short runs.
No more mounted troops in blind obedience rush
As in "The charge of the Light Brigade"
But a planned blitz with tanks and PCs of heavy armour
Stiff resistance to break
Punching lanes and corridors for the light armours and men
Their own entry to make
The left overs to rake and mop.
No phalanx marshalled on the plains only for the foe to see
But troops camouflaged and phalanx only for the ships at sea
No wastage of men and planes in desperate Kamikaze
But stealth, drones and cruise attacks with no craze!
No slow maneuvering ducks in the sky
But supersonic fighters tripple gravity twisters!
No more need the sky to scan for the big birds with the bombs;
For the stealth has dropped its load and gone
Long before your upward gaze.
Enough of the runs with targets missed
For the bombs have gone too smart to tease
Surely; down in his grave Nelson grins and marvels

Watching the Subs maneuvering in the seas.
And soon from bases up in space, Moon and Mars
The lands of the earth could be hit and burnt
The oceans of the world to burning sulphur turned.
New breading stock in Noah's flood ship survived
But what ship can a burning sea sail
For fauna and flora to survive?
What will be left unscorched
From fires from three thousand bangs?

NATURE COUNTRY
LIFE AND SEASONS

MY ROOTS—YEAR 1960 AD

Where I did sprout
Among the hills and mountains
Valleys and fast running rivers and brooks
There are:
No asphalt surfaced streets; tidy kerbs
Manicured lawns, with flower beds.
No tree dotted green parks
but sandy grounds for lasses and lads
No tall street lamps, street names, public taps.
No hedge-lined side-walks
and athletes on morning jogging.
No play-house; no cinema; no pubs
Just a drinking few in the brewer's court.
No serious crimes; no cops; no law court;
Since ethos, taboos and ostracism scare the hearts of all.
No Newsstands; no telephone booths
Town crier that's all!
No center for Medicare
Just a drugstore and a herbalist's
barks, leaves and roots junk room, at the market square.
No mechanic; no radionics
Just a watch and a bicycle repair shed
Of an old man *Alago* and mister *Alekesandar* his friend.
No dusty winds; nor steamy heat
No level plains, but rolling hills
No visiting hostile winds,
But gentle mountain breezes.
No war, no strife
Just little knotty disharmonies
O, nature clad village!
You will hold my roots
When next I come.

THE BLACKSMITH'S SHOP

Oseni's workshop
A small rickety structure wedged between boulders
Atop the northern shoulder
of a range called the goat hill.
A small building
Half way between a house and a hut.
For it was mud walled, grass thatched
Just like most other houses then.
Larger than a hut
But smaller than a house for sure.
It had an entrance but no frame nor door.
Three fenestrations; two on the village side
And the other looking into the thorny hillside.
Oseni's workshop had no rooms,
For he did not live there obviously.
His home, a stone throw away,
Just after the streets intersection
Where there were always some totems of sacrifice
Was a much more comfortable edifice.
With a veranda and four rooms that were accessed
from a common lobby, which also served as
The reception, living room, dining and a meeting place of pride
For the village's growing "elites"
A female group that met every fortnight
And to which Oseni was the patron.
On the uneven walls
were two photo wall-mats and a clock
That was right twice a day
Everyday!
There were also two almanacs
An old one of nineteen twenty-two;
And a more recent one of fifty-two
Just a decades ago!
Each room of ten by ten had

A window of buckled wood
That opened briefly during a search
for a needle, dropped coins and the like.
Oseni's workshop
Rated the largest factory in the locality,
Churned out hoe blades, cutlasses, arrowheads,
Knives, sickles, seed-yam slicers,
Game-traps and water-well pail retrievers
Of the highest quality!
I did work many hours after school in Oseni's factory
Rhythmically stroking those large lungs;
Those large tough bellows
for the price of a small initials-branded personal knife
Girls had no business in this workshop,
Except on two occasions when they came for
The fixing and removal of the heavy copper bridal bangles
Which of course could only be done personally
by Oseni
Perhaps for certain personal satisfaction
Linked to the reaction of the frightened, most-times struggling
brides.
Now the banging is gone
From the once vibrant works.
No rhythmic puffing comes
From the large lungs of Oseni's furnaces
His skills no longer cope
With time's fast strides.
As for the brides
They are at peace as you know
With the ever changing times.
Their arms do not have to be weighted
For submission!!
Not at all; not at all
They do not have to be weighted
Since love's sacred grotto
must have long been breached severally
Before the supposed night of pain and sweetness.

DISPERSAL

One by one, with sharp cracking noise
The pods pried open, in the intense tropical sun
Flinging seeds far away, from their cozy beds.
Some into the fast flowing brook fell
Floating; buoyed by their oily flaps while
others in diverse bowels later would ride
And so to different terrains dispersed.

Fluffy feathered seeds from numerous open buds
Of the wild lint cotton tree, rise like minute Harriers
From the floating decks of some carriers
Into the sudden surge of breeze,
Or a great gust of passing wind
Riding the flow like some Lilliputian troops
Dropping to ground in their micro chutes.

As I watched from under some tree shade
The unfolding spectacles; the memory tape of history rewound
As I remembered the colonies in turn
And the era, when *Britannia ruled the waves*.
How men in the manner of these seeds made their ways
Or loaded and shipped to these lands far away
America; Australia; New Zealand;
Canada; Gibraltar; Zululand.
And then I remember my seeds too
Nursed, and to some high degrees schooled.
All dispersed as it were overtime
By land water and air
Many now embedded for life
In the new lands and climes.
Leaving empty, these rooms of our palatial home
That we built with different thoughts and hopes.

ECHO FROM THE MOUNTAIN

I take my stand to make the shout
Like women of old seeking reassurance and blessing
As they rest their weary limbs here
on their way to distant markets.

I make my shout
And hear your voice echo mine
Flowing back to me and turning round
back into the rocks thinner and thinner.
Taking me along into the darkness of your body,
To grope my way back, or lost forever.

I sway and shiver as the cold shower
of the past runs over me.
For in this Echo-land, I have made my calls
And now wait for the tide to sweep in
And back into the future.

ENHANCED

Never labour for a mere 'Hercules' boy!
Old farmers ride this bike
All of last year's batch of migrant labourers
Have just returned in time for Christmas,
Invading the streets
Re-establishing areas of influence
Weakened by their absence
A dozen and half months in the plantations
In the cocoa and cola-nuts plantations
Of the south west.
And my trump when I return is
A brand new "Rudge" or
A'Raleigh' bicycle with
A high sounding handle-bar bell
My arrivals to announce
As I cruise the village streets and lanes.
Then that tall dark apple of my eye
Shall fall freely
Like an over ripe mango fruit
At the lightest shake of the tree.
My status enhanced
My influence renewed.

NEW YAM

Now that my eyes have seen you
I shall no longer die.
No longer die, and for the third and last time
I say, I shall not die.
You fill my heart with happiness
My eyes with tears of joy.
We have waited for your arrival
On the season's snail slow coach.
Waited for this day of hope
While we exhumed un-sprouted seed-yams
for the fire
Drowning the crumbs in gourd of water
Listening to the rhythm of our visceral splashes.
The child waited too!
Waited for the stone buried as yam
In the hot embers to soften
Until sleep brings a new day.
With this touch of you
I touch my chest.
Once, twice, thrice!
And I say
I have seen you savior
I shall no longer starve.

TO THE SCORPION

Who dares to ride your saddled back, nocturnal raider.
Who strolls too near your saddle
Guarded by this severally re-usable missile.
Un-camouflaged
Raised high for deterrence and
Permanently on red alert!.
Terror arachnid; the light of day you loathe
While blitzing all the night through,
Destroying foes for food.
Inflicting pain when death is beyond your use,
At the slightest brush.

But then; for every poison, an antidote,
Every venom, an anti-venom
Every missile, an anti-missile system
Every Goliath, a David.
And your conqueror
A cute little mammal
That outwits your darting strikes
Delivering its vicious bites
at the mid-section of your missile
Disabling its mechanism for flight
Or strike.
Killing you.

HARMATTAN

The heavy morning haze
Shrouded the tree tops
The distant village huts
In a blanket of dirty white.
Ahead; half the street disappears
Swallowed in this suspended flow
Cloaking approaching figures ghostlike.
Up in the East,
The sun, heavily shrouded even at eight,
Cannot make its way
To stoke up its oven and warm the shivering earthlings.
Happy at the hapless sun
The wind breaks loose from its tethers
It's cold penetrating teeth, it's claws unsheathed
Naughtily rushes around
Hissing
Biting,
Clawing.

On the streets, smile-less faces gaze.
Their greetings crawling through slightly opened lips
Teeth barely visible
For that is the height of caution
To spare the lips those painful cracks
of the blood filled, caked grooves.
Grooves latent like midget dormant volcanoes
Waiting to crack open
at the opportune moment releasing new flows.

On the brown fields
Grasses, leaves and twigs tinder dry
Ready and willing collaborators with
Any careless smoker's live stub
half crumble underfoot.
Cracking
Disintegrating
Raising mushroom clouds of dust
As you walk through.
Harmattan!
But soon it will be over
And the sun will reign supreme
For a couple of months when the rains resume
For all lives—flora and fauna
To bloom and roam again.

A VILLAGER AND THE CITY NIGHT SKY

There is a sky
Just as blue at night
A moon
Just as full and sweet
Some trillion sparkling stars
I found them yesterday
Just yesterday!
My neighbours lost a season ago.

THE OWL

Your name truly sounds despair.
Your face of mask a child would scare.
Your plumage an unhappy grey,
Your throaty calls, real *caveat* to your preys
We fell the *Iroko* tree of the forest fringe.
We cut the tall palm trees that dotted the village streets.
Yet you come, bearer of doom.
Perch not on my roof
Just go yonder and give us relief
Go to them where they live
And perch on their roofs.
Those who can see the back of their necks

THE ANT HILL

Has none in wisdom search
Pried into this multi-minaret edifice
This epitome of orderliness and industry
Of tradition and loyalty
For cures for our ills
The ills of nature's leading creature?

RETIREMENT

Now will I listen to the town crier
And the pulpit preacher.
No longer entirely to the radio talker
And the television, with its programmed lies.
Now will I watch the kids on the village play grounds
on lovely moon drenched nights,
And not some violence laded video films and movies.
Now I can rest in the open courtyard of my home
Or there at the unguarded frontage
Un-caged.
Asleep.
Gone with the tranquilizing breeze
Until matins; when the chill sends me in.

I will savour daily henceforth
Real appetizing native cooking
Not ruined with chemical spices and the kind
Served in some homely earthenware
The calabash or wrapped in leaves!
Move away from the city's bottled drinks
But in to the native brew and the palm wine
Poured into spherical calabash drinking bowls
Sand scrubbed and washed creamy white,
sun dried.

Truly, no more knife and fork and
No chop sticks for sure.
I will strip me down to my waist
Savouring my meals, licking the fingers in turn
At ease and contented.
Away from the tension of those dining rooms and halls
The programmed smiles and laughter
Those designed coughing and talks.
I shall roast my pieces of yam

On wood fires with golden embers
Dipping each slice or piece
in freshly homemade palm oil
And scooping the brownish oil dreg
with hot crusty lumps.
My homemade bread and butter so to say.

There I can attend ticket free
Nature's orchestra in reserved seat
Royally cushioned with leaves and twigs
In the cozy shade of some majestic trees
deep in the forest by a stream.
Filling each self-imposed recess thumbing these beads
Crowned with the crucifix.

For variety,
I may comb the derived savanna plains
Toil up slope of mountains
Traversing the ranges far and near,
Stalking the alert mountain deer
And that sharp squeaking mammal with no tail.
Walking back home tired but happy
With or without a trophy.

HIBERNATION

What kept you alive
Under this sandy shady stretch
Of our mountain river bed
Your sacred place of quiescence
these past many months.
You endured the long dry season
With strength beyond all reasons,
But failed to truly sense the early season flow
That barely covers the river floor ankle deep
From the flow of the heavy continuous falls.
Hence your hurried emergence
To this unprotected experience,
Splashing and splashing;
Swimming nose to tail
Upstream
Your large bodies barely submerged.

Locals;
Catch not the leading *Agun* fish.
For the gods forbid it
Since tomorrow must know their fate
When their leader narrates the tale
Of their emergence swim.
But all the others in toe
All the splashing fish behind
Are manna from Mother Earth.

RIVER NIGER FROM THE AIR

How long did your early labour last
To fruit to this meandering silvery ribbon?
How long was that early flow
That cleaned your lengthy bowel
To this settled shimmer?
How long will it take for mine
To cut its desired illuminated path
Across this difficult terrain?

NIGHT ERRAND

I hummed a song to scuttle my fear
Half running, half walking towards the market square
Through which I would traverse
To *Kila* the hunter's home.
Kila, the hunter and high priest.

Pitched black and drizzling
The distance doubled as it were.
Stretched out
by the elastic fibres of my fear.
My head felt ballooned
Pumped near busting by the bottled fear in my chest
My neck cricked under the added weight of my loaded head
As the market square I neared.

All quiet.
Loudly quiet
As I approached the market square.
This village is dead.
Like the day now cloaked in darkness.
No bleating goats.
No barking dogs.
Nobody!
Dead.
Without a speck of light
This village, which will spring to life
Hours before the sun rises, is dead.

My steps quickened as the two silhouette drew nearer
One his house, and the other, his shrine
The drumming heightened in my chest
Propelling me into a short burst
Right to his covered entrance.
And I called in panic
Baba Kila!!

BAR BEACH LAGOS

What stirs this vastness to limitless joy
What forces, beneath or above
Rule this seething; this watery tumult
Revolting or rejoicing as it were
Like that city there behind me.
Tell me mermaid.

LAMENTATION OF THE GODDESS OYI

"Omorohun my daughter!
Daughter of the river great in flood
Omorohun, O Omorohun my daughter
Every time it rains
Every time it floods
I shall send from my heart to you
Messages of love; every time it rains
Omorohun my daughter
Daughter of Oyi in great floods"

This we heard from up in the sky
As Oyi who lost her daughter wailed across the sky
Back to the river from where she came
Mourning the death of her daughter Omorohun
Who died that day in the deep of a river.

Gorgeous goddess
Whose beauty astounded all gods around
Who showered encomiums
through fast tumbling streams.
She had sent her only daughter to the home
Of an industrious goddess that lived in the depth of *Oboto*
A revered stretch on the river *Ohe*
Flowing through the valleys of Ogidi.

And so it was on a market day
Goddess *Oboto* had left her cares.
Away to sell her wares
When fishers come and raided her home.
A cut off dam was thrown across some width
To ring the niche that was her home.

Great was the efforts of *governess Tilapia*
Who scuttled around to check her wards
But soon got caught in one of such rounds
As the fishers drained the water
that was her cover.
Then all were caught along with Omorohun
Daughter of the goddess of river *Oyi*.

She hurt her left big toe on a stone
A small sturdy protrusion right in the clearing
where the market held.
"No not at noon and the market full
What could it be; what signal, what omen"
She jettisoned her fears
And stayed to sell her wares.

There upon a table rock
Laid the fairest of all.
Since the fishermen were six
Five plus one dissenting voice,
She was cut into five
The tail and head to make up seven.
The tail and the head for the little fool
That begged for a halt and stood aloof
On hearing the wail coming from the water of *Oboto*
The abode of Omorohun.

Oyi came down fast and together with *Oboto*
they wept inconsolably
For the loss of the beautiful daughter of *Oyi*,
The river goddess.
As they wept, the heavens opened
And the river rose
The flood widened, trapping and sweeping away all but
The dissenting boy lifted up by the goddesses in grief
And perched on the fork of a tree.
The flood spread

Sweeping all their catch back
Into the deep of Oboto, leaving Omorohun
cut into seven now turned into stones
All there to this day.

"Omorohun my daughter!
I go home now alone, all alone.
Leaving you here turned into stone.
I shall send messages to you, stone child
From this heart full of grief
Every time it rains
Omorohun my daughter; the fair one
Daughter of the river; seven brooks in one
I shall send back tributes
Though you live now as stone."

And then in the recent past
With crosses and crucifix in hand,
A new group came and fished.
But their catch would not boil.
The pieces turned and groaned in the pots!
So they went round the town
Dancing, clapping, chanting thus
"Groan if you like
Turn if you like
Fish from Oboto groan if you like
What we caught is nothing but fish
Groan if you please"

Fish groaned in the pots
Turning, struggling as they would not cook
Fish swept back by flood
Back into Oboto will surely never cook
For all the gods decreed it so
That, we are told

MOONLIGHT NIGHT

Caress this body, gentle fingers
Let my heart feel your cool velvety touch
And carry me back the vista of years
When we hid and played behind those walls
Inside those rooms
Of the uncovered dilapidated house.
Singing, clapping
Acting our future lives
Mirroring our world.

Sweet moon and stars
Sweet play grounds
Where are those happy little feet?
Those varied tiny voices?
Where are they?
Dispersed and re-arranged
On the real stage?
Or still wishing?
Wishes fulfilled?
Or dead in reality?

I see them now with these eyes inside me
Hear the voices cutting across these years unchanged
Unchanged like the moon's face unwrinkled by age.
Dear moon, dear stars
Dear sands
Streets and grounds.
Dear little fathers
Little mothers
Wives and children.
Dear friends
Dear chiefs
Priests
Masquerades, and slaves
Dear nights.
When again can we meet together
To reminisce?
To savour.

A MAN IN THE RAIN YEARS AFTER CHILDHOOD

Run down my head
My chest; my back
Down between my legs
Soothing!
Touch my ribs caressing fingers of water
Loving tenderness come down.
Come down more dear rain.
Faster still and fill these cupped palms again and again
To quench my thirst?
No!
To drink to my luck for this treat
This special childhood gift.
So come down enough sweet rain
Again to brush my brow, my face
And spit the excess in sprays of joy.
No winds.
Just come and numb these fingers of mine.
Shrink them wrinkled and white
Shrink it too down there!
Roughen this hairy possession of mine
In a million goose pimples
Reducing it to a receding stump!
Then lead me back home in drunken steps
Now that I cannot run the streets
Splashing the pools
In the joy of your visit.

GOOD BYE CENTER
OF EXCELLENCE

An amorphous mass
A planning mess
A city of ten thousand stinking garbage hillocks
Each infested by a wretched group of foraging poor
Each armed with a metal crook and carrying a sagging trophy sack
Thrown across one shoulder.
O "Center of excellence"
How truly excellent you are.

"City of aquatic beauty"
Not like in that state with ten thousand lakes
Up there in the States
But that of a great lagoon network
Daily polluted by tones of untreated human and industrial wastes.
Corpses and carcasses litter your streets days unattended
Worsening further the already uncomfortable humid tropical air
O Lagos
How beautifully captivating you truly are!

The sick and destitute roaming your streets
Emphasize to the admiring world
Your generosity to your own folks and all
In alms giving, disease sharing et al.
Great indeed is your national and international sympathy
For you open wide your mercy gates to
Grotesquely disabled lots and
The amputees of the rigid and unmerciful Sharia courts
Hungry curly haired beggars
From beyond our unguarded northern frontier
Confirm most strongly your worthy title
"Center of excellence" and I add
"Defender of the defenseless"

You beat the world 'am proud to say
In road pot-hole count per kilometer stretch.
In streetlight poles the vital parts removed.
In traffic lights that never blink.
In Avenues of bill boards and not trees.
Tangled mass of burnt out or accident vehicles
And disused cars and trucks from yester years
Adorn your roads and streets.
Upstaging the killing field
Of The Kuwait city road
The road of the Iraqi escape bid
Of the "Desert storm" war.
Surely Lagos
You can't be more captivating

Your beaches "Center of excellence"
Captured from tourists,
By hoards of habit wearing, cross bearing natives
Weakened by fasting and a thousand Alleluia
Beckon to a negative re-visit.
While the bulging reddened eyes and erratic dancing
Of street urchins at the periphery of the sand
Ring out a loud caveat.

O Lagos
Behold the imposing edifice of
Your "Environment monitoring group",
Located most prominently with the clearest of views
Its windows gazing
At two gigantic steel and iron recycling plants amid homes
Covering residents with lethal dust.
Your city chemical plants
Numerous foam processing plants
Fumigate your people at will.
How much you truly care
Great "City of excellence"

How sweet to hear this reflex blaring
From your trucks, cars and bikes.
The amplified canvassing
By your army of garage touts.
The ceaseless jangling from roadside works
Scores of competing rowdy music
From terraced cubicles of your shopping areas.
The madness form hundreds of praying houses
From private mosques and mushroom churches;
Whose croaking chocking prayers fill our nights
Wrecking our sleeps, our rests, and
Confusing our already tortured minds.

Lagos, "Center of excellence"
Do I love the madness in your life?
The bus drivers maneuvering recklessness
Their conductors drunken restlessness
The traffic warden's sadistic excesses.
The leaching police's disgusting brazenness
The emergency vehicles deceptive bravado.
Fire engines jangling, hooting, snaking through the traffic
A full one hour after the conflagration!
The ambulances on no mission of mercy
Blaring through the traffic already stalled!
Armoured vault trucks bashing,
Crashing their way through
Their armed escorts threatening
Lashing out with guns and whips
Snaking in and out of lanes sirens shrieking
And to the kerbs many motorist veered crashing.

O Lagos
Did I forget the street pests called the "Area Boys"?
Street urchins!
What elegant public relation officers of
The "Center of excellence" they are!
Then the boss of all
The armed robbers

Ruling the day and the night.
With all these dear Lagos
I truly admire your great courage
In announcing to the world and displaying
Vehicle number plates and tags
"Lagos Centre of Excellence and Aquatic Beauty"
I will surely not miss you Lagos
As I retire to my village home
Deep in nature's garden.

TOWN CRIER

A little raised ground at the town center
is his cherished spot.
A starting point where his view is clear
And the voice can spread.
He strikes his signature tune
Three spaced strokes.
Then a sharp burst of rapid clangs
Of penetrating gong sound
That carried to all around.

"Shut up all of you
Do you hear me?
You!
I mean you"!

The narrator heard.
The song and clapping stopped
And up in the sandy square
The wrestling stopped.
All stood rooted to their spots
Bathed in the rich flood
Of this bright moonlight night.
Again the gong peeled
This time in regular beats
Then stopped.
And the voice came
Cutting across the silenced night
Linking with words, royal and subjects' minds.

CLIMATIC CHANGE

From the tilted trays of heaven
Hailstones, for brief periods often hit
Our play grounds; our homes
With sudden accelerating clatter.
And the ricochets from the zinc roofs scatter
With no vicious mission, submitting rapidly
Like their play-ground traveling mates to some watery end.

We did on the farm tracks in mornings pick
After a night of heavy pour, crabs, prawns and fish
Flown down to ground I suppose
From the rivers in the clouds
In the chariot of the pouring rains and whistling storms.
On our lush plains; fruitful forests and green rolling ranges
We did hunt and farm.
In great swamps, Fadama lands,
Rice and other early crops did thrive.

Now the trays tilt no more
For the hail stones to fall
Since not enough hails a tilt to cause.
And so many men below forty
Falling hails in our land have never seen.
Nor have they a fish or crab picked
While jogging or playing on the fields.
Familiar now are the aborting soils
Dwindling forest lands, and thirsty caking valued swamps.
Phoebus we are told
Keeps stoking his ember-filled oven
And must be appeased before he bakes to char this land;
While melting some and others he drowns.

EILAT—ISRAEL

I have sailed on Mungo Park's lordly Niger
Down the grasslands, forests and swamps.
I have been to the great Niagara and seen
The parade of flowers in colours in
Great gardens and parks.
I cherish the captivating scenes
Of my tropical homeland
The fascinating beauty
Of our teaming grasslands
Deserts and marshlands
Serengeti, Masaimara
Luangwa, Okavango et cetera
And now this under water world of Eilat.
This watery teaming home of some of nature's
Non-parell of creatures
This flowing elegance
Whose closeness and variety is its fragrance.
Many times I have shuddered with delight and awe
At the share immensity and beauty of nature
But never have I viewed with unbridled reverence
Such gracefully unfolding display.
Never witnessed such colourful parade
Of nature's select teams
Flowing in this Red Sea niche
Eilat.

DEPARTURE FROM THE COLONY

Perhaps in obedience to a royal order
What was a trickling exit
Quickly became a frenzied transit
Out of the citadel
Into the darkness of the night.
The cool night following the early evening down pour
The night of the proclaimed nuptial flight
As million engaged lovers
With cupid's loaned temporarily stitched wings
Took to the air in love pairs
The future kings and queens of new found lands
The abodes thus built by the surviving colonists
Are clones of their native ant hill
In orderliness and industry
In dedication and loyalty to state
A lesson for us at the apex
Of heaven's creation to emulate.

BETROTHAL

Let his kindred come
Uncles, sisters, aunts.
Let them come
and kneel with him.
Prostrate.
Let me hear their chattering voices
The joyful discourse, of their common intent.
Let the excitement grow out there
and invade the serenity of this room.
Let is drown the drumming from my chest
Erase the intermittent whispers
Of my guiding aunt.

"Just clear enough
Do you hear?
Clear enough dear girl.
Delay your response just a little.
A little suspense, just a little"

"I hear Auntie"
Let me savour the beauty of their voices
All for me; seeking me.
Seeking to hear that they already know.
The "Yes I will" they know must surely come.

"Quiet, quiet everybody!
Quiet everybody!"

Quickly woman leader
Pop the question and have your answer.
Your answer.
This lump stuck in my throat.
Get it out and set me free.
Let loose the jubilation.

The ululation
That ancient wail of joy
Awulele
From the well drilled throats
Of our crowd out there

Three special bursts of joy
For him and for me.
Now shall I accept the *ekejo*
The woven symbol of betrothal
But pray it is that adorned with cowries
And not with hole-in-the-heart pennies
That I might reap the ancient blessings
Of our noble past.

THE FARMER AND THE TSETSE FLY

Please fly tsetse fly.
Why drill on these eggs?
Why there between my legs?
I will cry please fly.

I will suck where I like
So strike if you wish
Death on the throne is a worthy death
Death elsewhere is a bloody mess
Now strike if you like,
For when I feed I do not fly.

Do I scrape with the knife
The child's faeces on my skin?
Will she shout into the night
And expose the crime; the hideous sin;
The king and maid in the dead of night?
No.
A quiet moan and push; a gentle fight
So off!
I shall not strike.
Since your death from my strike is so unsure
And hit or miss I'll surely hurt.

BAT INVASION

Shredded palms
Depleted foliage
Naked arms outstretched and skywards
In silent protest.
Now the exposed middle class afraid to prosper
Fearing devastation
Struggle through the skeletal arms
Of defoliated larger trees.
Thousands of "winged fruits" droop
In solemn retreat.
Tens of thousands in festive flights
Crisscrossing in the air
Dampen further this late noon light
In *Irun town* and its devastated forest

TO THE BAT

How do you chart your way
Through this night and the dark cave?
Through this dense surrounding world of trees
Why do some of you droop
From the forest woods
In sober retreat
While others come and go
In joyous excitement?
Will an inspirational droop like yours
Lead me to this excellence
To chart my course
Through this world like yours?
Tell me bats.

THE PLAYMATES RETURN TO BASE

A few only, returned to the stage.
All that was left of the age group.
A group of a dozen and half merry kids
That those narrow alleys roamed and
Those small cubicles of
The uncovered mud house by the playground occupied
In games of hide and seek, and marriages
on moon drenched nights.
Nights that were masquerades free
Just few hours before bed.

The remnants of our cast were home.
Brought back on stage for the coronation
Of one of theirs, a playmate on the sand
As the village head and head of clan.
Home too, was the memory of them
That have left the big stage truly dead.
Their sweet carefree faces curling across the sky,
fleeing with the shooting stars.
We have become the ancient cast
Wrinkled and grey.
We are the vanishing species they say
And soon like the receding watery glitter
before the lonely desert traveler,
Our era shall be gone.

Our songs and folklores are heard no more
Our games, our moonlight plays are dead and gone
In their stead are karaoke machines,
Video games and
DVDs, in rooms and parlours.

The streets, the alleys no longer dark
When the trillion stars go to hide,
Or the moon and the rain clouds connive.
For the bulbs hanging from some poles
Ensure that holy order
Let there be light
Is re-enacted over and over every night.

For perhaps my last time, I say Adieu
Dwindling village square
Adieu again dear wrestling grounds
Lovely sands
Kind to the knees, heads, and elbows at fall.
To you too ancient trees and
Stone seats of the market place
Vultures on scavenging flights up in the sky, adieu
Goats, sheep and dogs, roaming the streets.
The slurry ponds, the garbage dumps and their pigs.
Adieu free ranging chicken of the yards
And the line of wobbling doodling ducks.
Adieu too, modern kids with your modern crazes
Your borrowed cultures
Your funny gabs and weird dances
Look! There in the horizon I can see those
Who your cherished acts and ways
Will for sure to the archives consign.
Just as ours to the dead you have re-assigned.

YOUR LOSS

The sun moved behind the hills
Splashing the horizon with
Gold, crimson red and other colours
The last show of the dying day.
But there is time
And yams went on the fire.
Suddenly a change and the day is dead.
We were tricked again!

The echoes of distant calls
Announcing or checking departures.
Knotted bunches of grass,
Broken twigs, or just leaves.
Seven pebbles on a small heap of sand at farm path junctions.
All signs of mates that have left for home.

Then, the growing darkness.
The bats charting courses between the trees of the forest
hardly visible.
The fire flies.
The unnerving noise of night life
The owls!
The cheeping insects and birds.
Then the sudden rustle from the under growth
Of animals escaping
That sends one missing a step!
That blood chilling darkness deepened
tropical smell of the forest at night.
The sound of your own steps
And the hard imaginary steps at the rear

Setting the hairs erect!
The approaching ghost like figure!
You slow down
Causing the line to collapse on you.
Then a swear or two
Or a spank!
Over all these; the tirade at home for coming late
These and others my child
You have missed.

OLAGA—CULTURAL MAID DANCER

When I think
Of how these white stained hands and minds
Caused your slow and painful death
In this land of your birth
I weep.
When I think
Of how these crusted myopic eyes of mine
Saw but shame and nakedness in
Your beauty, your elegance
That I now cherish in the hazy form
I see and remember,
I weep.

The plotters with me of your death
Now sing your praise
And call on me to exhume your remains
Re-cast your multifaceted ways of life.
But where do I dig?
Where do I search
For your grave; your scrolls dear Olaga?
Buried as it were not in one but thousand caves and graves
In some million homes
In every royal court of the land
In every shrine of the gods
In the depth of the unstained hearts
Now dead with you.
Where do I dig?
What do I do to bring you back dear Olaga?
There is a country I am told
Where the spirits of the dead invoked

Are seen and heard.
They might, if the rite is performed
Come back to live with us again.
Dear *Olaga*
Will you come to live with us again
And not rehearse the tantalizing visit
you paid your kith and kin
When they made their call at FESTAC seventy-seven
In a city called Lagos?

DEVASTATED FAUNA

Then on her laps she said I laid suckling.
When stampeded bush hogs in dozens
Across the village square and between the houses
Came rushing in confused flight
Causing great commotion and fear in the fading light.
Then into the forest and up the mountain; all lost
but a few hacked down or shot.
"And indeed another unexpected visit there was
shortly after", mama said
"When hundreds of large horned animals came hoofing across
Just beyond the village perimeter
Where now there sit a school and a church"

Great sanctuary was this land now so devastated.
Very common were road signs by the British erected
On the few dirt roads in this domain of large herds
Calling for caution.
"Buffaloes and Elephants Beware", some cried.
"Lions and Big cats Territory" warned others.
But now, nothing crosses these roads on ground but in the air
Butterflies, birds, bats bees and ants!
For all those treasured fauna of Africa South
That in abundance once did roam here
Have in most of our land disappeared
Hunted into extinction by our men.

DOCUMENTARIES— HIDDEN DANGERS

Danger locks unobserved in the air
In water and indeed resides everywhere.
In the gentle breeze it rides unseen
Its fangs, its claws; its fearsome set of teeth
Away from feeding, grazing or resting eyes sheathed
But unfrocked sometimes by nostrils keen
When scent from gliding breeze do seep.
Or eyes half-awake from misty sleep
Or a lucky glance from frenzy engagement.

Flowing tears from clouds in sorrow mourning
Drenching the hills for days
Melting their tough skins; their hard cores
With mud slides down the valley go rushing.
Clogging roads, streets, invading homes, causing deaths.
.
Angry rivers filling the valleys
Flooding the plains
Overrunning the streets
Gliding un-announced into homes
Evicting,
Flushing out all and sundry
In style and manner most inconsiderate.

In the belly of the mountain; its peaks majestic
With garment of velvet green its slopes adorning
Lies a lake of fire in angry storm a vent searching.
And then in deep frustration de-cones the mountain
Spitting death in ash and gaseous fountain
Darting massive tongues of liquid fire; flapping over the lips
Cascading down the slopes
In river of cruel cremating.

Swiveling between depressed stained fingers is
a potent danger.
Briefly glowing; feigning dead; glowing again
Lazy smoke coiling away and
The fainting glow leaking to the base.
Glowing at the last pull; the last feign
And the careless ejection from the smoker's fingers
Into the leaves and grass so tinder.
Weakly comes back to life
A crinkling gently smoldering fire.
To a roaring massive spreading conflagration
That for days raged, causing destruction.

LOVE AND PASSION

MARIGOLD AND THE NATURE LOVER

I am Marigold
A Marigold from a garden bed
Dislodged and cast over fence
By careless hands and wicked mind
Mid-day, and wilting.

I am a nature lover
Roaming the country wide
Searching for nature's prides.
Passing along the garden path
Were you laid.
Laid among the weeds and thorns,
And yet conspicuous.

Conspicuous?
Conspicuous with my fallen petals,
My twisted stem and withering leaves
Among the harsh bush and thorns?
No, not conspicuous.

Yes Marigold
Conspicuous like the moon and stars
Playing hide and seek with the patchy clouds
On a moody night.
Like a lost pet at dawn carrying a jingle
An unmarked stolen car a homer installed.
A white man painted black
On a noon parade among a line of Bantus.
Conspicuous; yes dear, conspicuous.

Then hide me.
Nature lover; hide me
From unwary heels of the trodden path.
From the drought and fire
That plague the bush around the garden fence.
From the hungry sickle
That knows not the wild 'gold
from the garden 'gold
When not where it should be.
Hide me please, nature lover; hide me.

I will Marigold
And take you along with me
To fill the missing slot
on my nature's jig saw puzzle;
The missing gem, on my precious mosaic.
I shall make you a new bed
Rich and clumpy; full of moisture.
And since it is noon
And the heat from the sun is strong,
I shall bid the sun not to stand still
As it did over Gibeon
But hurry away under a clock; and let my plant take.
Let it take and bloom again.

WAIST BEADS

Arousing elegance!
Hidden from unwelcome stares.
Whose silhouette the eyes and heart excites
Are to me like Hawaiian garlands
Around the neck of treasured tourist
to that nature's paradise.
A crown of flowers on the proud head
Of a *Victor Ludorum.*
The unique fragrance of these bands of beads
Which surely is not perceivable by nasal sensors
But seeps through the eyes permeating the entire body;
When from her heart she does presents
Or in taunting movements flashes!
This garland
This crown of beads atop the love grotto
This enhancing beauty of the midst,
Always sends my pump running high
Raising most elegantly the flow
In all vessels of my body; my groins!
As she rushes past me or
Jumps off to escape my love grabs
The sensuous jiggling bead sound;
Like that enticing sound from rushing brook water,
Cascading, shifting, rolling pebbles on pebbles
Adds fuel to the fire of my love
The glowing embers of my desire.

TRAILING THE TROUPE

I want a girl
Just as tall and dark
With plaited hairs
Shoulders low
A set of teeth
That shows the heart.
An ample lightly rocking pair on chest
Firm to touch.
A waist of beads
Navel high.
Unblemished props
Full to base.
Like that lead girl there
Of the dancing troupe.

MY WIFE AND MY VISITING FRIEND—THE MUSE

When the muse, my ear, mind and spirit engage
My wife of course, for that period so intimate exists divorced!
When in our home; muse's fragrance she perceives,
She hesitates the door to knock, or if ajar proceed;
The peace and moments of inspirations discompose
There with me, this elegant gifted daughter of Zeus
Dares my queen, for my attention to compete.
And humbly, the upper hand my wife concedes
For those lengths of time
After which divorce is reversed with a smile of peace.

VALENTINE

Thirteen cupid's arrows shot
On this dreamy valentine's day!
Two for sure I know
The other eleven flew in
Aimed from strong ambushing bows
Deep in the dense woods
Along this meandering path.
Thirteen piercing holes I think,
Will surely drain the over used passion fluid
In this forty-six year old pump.

FOLIORUM SILBULA—
FIRST COLLECTION

O *Foliorum Silbula* my companion, my friend.
Your conception and foetal life
three centuries stretched.
Three scores and seventeen was your age
When into this world I came.
But not withstanding my youthful age
Which stands at sixty-six,
Our love has blossomed surely to a craze!
Though you are multilingual,
I speak your mother tongue,
Which, though is in dialects of the past,
I slave to crack,
The sweet kernels there in, consumed at last
Foliorum silbula; your soliloquizing in Latin and Greek
I just can't comprehend
But that is unimportant to my mission:-
To stroll in this rich garden of poetic creations,
Embrace their elegance and
Listen to the eloquent voices of the British masters
Still ringing in the air.

Pope, Byron, Burns, Wordsworth, Dryden, Norton,
Spencer, WalterScott, Shakespeare, Logan Goldsmith, S. Johnson,
Campbell, Drumund, Coleridge, Tennyson,
Milton, Moore, Darlton, Ben Johnson,
Et cetera.
I flip with care *Foliorum Silbula*
Your rich pages, which fibres brittle with age,
Taping your tears
Mending your bruises with great care.
Your fate too I share
For my ageing fibres will soon begin to wear
Irreparably.
And like the masters of ages past
I'll succumb.

SILVER JUBILEE

With time petals fade and leaves turn brown
The bunch dries and crumbles away.
Hence you will not receive from me this day,
To mark our union day,
A bunch of flowers freshly cut,
Though all the wishes I send.
Sweetie,
I give to you from Cupid's garden fresh.
Bunch of love with petals of care
Buds of trust with fragrance pure
In vase of prayers to keep them fresh.
Since cupid grown, they never dry
Until death do us part

COME BACK

Scanty early season shower that sprouts to living green
Some forgotten seeds long roasted by the scourging sun
Last tiny sparks jumping from stone strikes on the cutlass head
Unto the fluffy soothy scrapings, from the base of the palm fronds
Setting a stack ablaze.
Rare fragrance of distance source, flowing in some lucky breeze
That wakes to stir, dormant senses the use near forgotten

The ground is loose to absorb
There is strength yet in the lungs
To widen the cancerous growth
Of this soothy fire to roar.
To clear the mucus waste for passage through
Of your sweet fragrance, to this bosom in need.

THE CROSS ROAD

The screen just would not clear
And different scenes still come and go
Scenes of happy days, of fun and love.
Of sour moods, and angry words too.
Surely the 'off button' has failed to function
Deepening the pain with new scenes replayed.
Pain of tearing, tumbling love.
Love until some time ago four lips did water
And tender fingers catered
Now lay wounded and drowning in our hearts.
Tossed here and there,
by strong winds of mistrust.
Frequently submerged
by fast under currents of anger.
Anger,
Of betrayed trust,
Of crippled decency.

Alea iacta est.
The die is cast
Yes; it is cast.
The curtain drawn
And the play achieved.
Forever.
My heart left to fallow
For many seasons to follow.
That the next crop might thrive
And fruit in bounty.

GOODBYE MY LOVE

We have laid these hearts side by side
For very many moons
And watched them throb and fuse
Until they beat in unison.
Producing in our blood
Some unbroken, vitalizing ripples.
But now that it be ripped
And each a half must take again,
I feel the tearing pain.
Adieu Carol
Adieu my *flame of the forest.*
Every time the thought of you returns
It is sweet and fresh
Like ageless Carols.

BONDING—FIRST BREAST FEED

Head bowed,
She adjusts and guides it through
The anxious un-accustomed lips.
Then the tiny eyes locked into hers unblinking.
Her eyes moved from head to toe; noting.
Then, setting back on the face.
Four eyes locked again and near visible rays
Bridged the space between the two
Bathing the child with beams of love

WO(E) MEN

I have seen it all around I swear.
For as long as the fires of her desires and cares
you poke and stoke as they come,
Your glances and words her commands become.
Her thoughts, her words, her actions
To you forever enslaved.
As sustenance efforts and other expectations wane
Glances become ray-less and words bounce away
Like maize grains
On an upturned calabash receptacle.
Your orders, now suggestion apparels wear.
Like a grafted citrus plant, a twin existence thrives
But not all of Eve's daughters this pet chameleon keep..
For there exist many,
Who in smooth brow or high gale
Labour on the sail with you.
Until it is land a-hoy!

OLD LOVER'S SONG

When plants wilt,
And leaves wither,
brown and fall.
When buds age,
The petals pale,
shrink and fade.
And then, the waiting compost base
They hug in final embrace
Presenting to the eyes, dull image
of past attractions; past allures.
Like leaves and petals of flowers
Eve's charming daughters too age
As all glow and beauty fade
When not with love, care and passion fed.
Then like petals dropping, down they go.

In my youth I loved to sing in praise
Of the freshness and the sweetness
of the freshly brewed.
But now I love and cherish in truth
The richness; the wholesomeness of vintage wine
Which flavour and satisfaction
grows with the mounting years.

Unlike the leaves and flowers that fade
And lose all beauty when they age.
Unlike some brews that with age go sour
You have blossomed and still maintain
The fragrance and freshness of a bud
With all petals and carpals displayed.
While your morning allure is still so much in place,

Your swan's gracefulness at youth
Has to a queenly carriage transformed.
And cupid in obedience to the gods, has with gentle care
Tinged with silver your crown,
That cascading luxury;
Which down to the nape and shoulders still rests.

Unlike the autumn aborting quickly
Its golden forest display before winter
Unlike the brief evening exhibition
of that priceless canvas
Of the setting sun's golden kiss
On the cheek of the western rim
Your radiance, cupid has decreed
Will continue to oil my heart and
Keep these eyes in love captivated
For the next one score and a half years
Bringing my sojourn here to a love soaked spectacle.

LOVE UN-ANCHORED

Now I know at last
My chameleon Saadat
That your love for me is truly fed and watered
By the compost heap and the vibrant spring
Whose sources deep down my pocket lay.
With this prolonged financial hiccup
Your love roams!
Flirting like the butterfly on daily calls
At different nectar pots.

WOMAN

Too many times
Since the first of cupid's arrows struck
Have I been cramped, gulped water
And almost drowned
Swimming in that treacherous pool
Of a woman's trust.
I have sank hip deep in the mire
Again and again
While reclining and often times free wheeling
In the booby trapped garden
Of woman's faith and trust.

My New Year resolution
The multiple babies
Of my annual end-of-year fast and abstinence
Delivered on the first day of each year
Have always had the gene transfer
For rejection
Or resistance
Of woman's trust; woman's faith.
But mutates during foetal formation and so
The new self remains the old!
Like yesterday that moults
Becoming today and tomorrow
But alas remains—a day!

And so like you, Sir Walter Scott
She spins me around her little finger nightly
Though I know, as you rightly professed
That woman's faith and woman's trust
Be written in the dust,
Stamped on the running water
Or printed on the moonlight's beam
"And each evanescent letter

Shall be clearer, firmer, better,
and more permanent I ween
Than the things these letters mean"
That the string of the promise of a maid snaps
When strained against the spider's thread.
And the plight of her heart
Weighs less than a grain of sand.
And yet Sir Walter
"I believe them again ere night"

THE DYING FLAME

Glance not now to disrupt; as on you I spy.
Consumed; lost in concentration as it were
In whatever your hands and mind engage.
Disturb not my flipping through the many pages
Of our radiant past
And the sluggish present compare.
Let these eyes and mind penetrate, range, and reflect
Back to base unhindered
Perhaps a pass would I locate
For passage through to
A fairer locale.

Why has heaven our thoughts not made for one another readable?
If only for thoughts and plans negative to our love to scan
While others, left as they are unaffected.
Then would all evils in the bud be nipped and
Lover's winter weather, to summer or spring transformed.
Strife of all shades and colours forestalled.

MARRIAGE

I know her now.
Well enough to make her mine
In joy and in pain
In sickness and in health
Until we part in death.
But really
I know not quite enough
Of whom I thought I knew.
For every day discoveries new!
New body
New mind
New likes and dislikes
A fathomless study
Until death do us part.

CHILD OF CUPID

I brushed this luxurious black crown
Back down the fine sculptured nape
Watching it recoil in its created waves
And felt the beats from this old pump
With greater ease come.
Oiled through these stroking fingers
With your fragranced grease.

I watched these two hillocks heaving.
Heaving to your gentle breathing
And thought of the simple love and care
That has bound together our pair
And wished to God in truth
That we remain firm and true
Like these lovely pair on you.

I watched your eyes as you slept
And saw the lashes in reflex quiver.
As I lightly kissed, you shivered
And I remembered what once you said
That "true love touch could wake the dead"
The peace of a child you wore.
The grace of an Angel was yours
Child of cupid
Deep in sleep.

WINTER BLIZZARD

What could stand in the path of
this devastating storms.
Blowing the past few months
Wrecking the elegance that our two hearts have built together
These many years.
The strong unending blizzard has blinded us
Sending us to diverging routes
Weakening our pumps and chilling
The warm flow of our veins;
Reducing us to immobile wrecks.

Spring! O Spring!
Come in fast and clear this chill.
Warm our bodies; warm our hearts.
Clear this storm that we may see
And move us on to summer's lanes
That our diverging routes
May again converge I plead.

A WAIST BEADS SOUVENIR

Two bands of the adorning quartet of
Your elegant waist,
As souvenir you lovingly expelled.
That I, your love left behind might
In sweet remembrance keep
That my anxious heart with yours in love be bound
Until your promised home return
With the Golden Fleece.
With this I surely will not severely miss
That sweet fragrance of your body
Since that has been richly absorbed and retained
By these beads you've had on for so long.
But then, incense to heaven I shall heavily burn
Throughout your stay of three seasons of summer sun
Since Medea's sorrows, her magical help you cannot receive
To charm, the dragon at the grove
For your entry there
And safe return home.

I WONDER

How much of your cherished heart dear Madalyn
is truly mine
And how much is his or theirs?
Those I do not and must not know.
How much is safely locked in there
Deep in the innermost recess
Behind those heaving busts?
How much do I really know
Or would ever know
About the flip side of your daily life coin
In hieroglyphic designed?
How many times in a day
Do I sincerely wish and pray
That the probing antennae of this anxious heart
Could sense and confirm with pride
The position and true depth of these exhibited emotions
The genuineness,
Of these romantic expressions.

THE VIRGIN'S SONG

Do not dilute the content of this bowl
The bowl of my native potion
Serve not with a thimble, glass, or mug
But drink from the bowl or
Straight from that gourd.
Then will you have the feel
The sweet joy
Of your intoxication.
Kiss not my lips
Or my body caress for
I am a native virgin from
deep down the jungle path
Clad only in beads around my mid.
So twist and smack me lovingly
Tickle me, tickle me and send me giggling.
I will scream and wriggle
Grab me and plead
Throw my arms round about me in a loving scuffle.
Wake me up and take me!
Take me whole.
All that you find
All that is me
For that is how it should be.

ADMIRATION

How many in her budding stage
Did her beauty appreciate?
In bloom; how many hearts
Got revved to peak mark
Merely by the sight of her close quartered
or just passing bye?
How captivating her frame!
How elegant her gait!
The grace and the beauty of Nefertiti
The charm, the mien of Cleopatra rolled into one
Is what I see through this covering mist
of time and age.
How truly I wish her clone be brought to life for me!
But since at her maturity I would have aged
I'll gladly produce a clone my place to take.
So that together as loving clones
Our lives we share.

AWAY IN TAIPEI

Send to me across these seven thousand miles
Your honey soaked voice if not your sunny smile
And bring back to life this starving heart.
Bid this object ring
Let it sing
And add our strand of love
To the thousands crisscrossing
in the air.
Bring the velvety lips of your soothing voice
To kiss my patched ears and heart.
Jump the seas
Skip the hills
And fall into the loving embrace
Of my heart.

DETACHING

With tenderness, and lots of care
I did prove my heart these years
To you that truly won my heart
Only to almost drown again and again
In the deep pool of the trust and love.
Pulled down by the strong undercurrent stirred up
By your clandestinely roving heart and life.
Rescued and recuperated this last time,
I turn my back on the wild wind one
The coquette that I have loved this long
For a cozy recline in the bosom of
The True Friend; True Love.

A YOUNG MAN'S VOW TO HIS SWEETHEART

When the sun and moon in final conflict tangle
And the moon in victory adds the day to her night
To rule all year round.
When the river Niger its flow reverses
And on Fou-ta Djallon source its water discharges
When hails fall on summer noon with nimbus not in sight
And the harmattan wind to snow blizzard turns
Then, might the thought with the blitz *come*.
Our love to abandon in the cold.

POLITICS

THE FLAG

Behold the Union Jack!
In peace and war the waves she ruled
With sweat and blood her flights sustained
At Waterloo; in Flanders field
In Falkland war; at Normandy beach
In the battle of Trafalgar
The Jack proudly flew.
O, take me back the vista of years
To the days of the Empire games at school.
The spirited drumming; the march past
The "eye-e-e-e-e-s right!"
As the salute platform we approached.
The Resident and then
The glorious anthem
As the Union Jack attained full height.
"God save our gracious Queen . . . .
God save the Queen."
The clapping
The joy of the day of our flag.

I love the Stars and Stripes
The great rallying force
Of "God's own country."
The moon welcomed her
And he stars embraced her again and again.
In the battle of the Bulge
With the pummeled, beleaguered garrison of Bastogne.
On Omaha beach and in
The "Hail Mary run" of the Gulf war.
The flag flew high!
Her children clutch her lovingly
Wrapping her round their sweat soaked bodies
Then flying her high in victory laps
Shedding tears of joy; of victory, on her
In arenas around the world.

From crest to crest of ranges bare
Across the desert from dune to dune
Standard and flag bearers brave barrages of fire
Along with fighting mates to plant
The white and blue with David's Star!
In cities; in Kibbutz the Star flies high
From tender ages her children know,
That the valves of their hearts are of David's star.

David's valve
Sustaining the flow
In the fighters of the Haganah
The six days war
The Yumkipur war!

And now to the Green-White-Green
My pride, my love, you'll think
And surely most would say—
Supposed to!
But, no.
My pride, yes; only in the stadia
When the goals are scored and races won.
Pretentiously,
When I am lined up in the sun
To wave the rigid plastic flag
To foreign dignitaries in convoys passing.

I hate the faded green of some of the flags.
I loathe their white turned brown
And masts with missing hosting strings.
My heart aches every time I see
My tattered flag drooping at barrack gates,
On government buildings all around,
And in some schools.
Flags, weather beaten; shredded
With tongues flying their different ways,
Like the swaying trashing arms of an octopus in flight
I see this vast country too
In the shredded flags we fly.

Who will kiss and weep with joy
holding you, rag flag?
Who will toil and spill precious blood for you
tattered emblem?
See now, the rain comes.
It is pouring fast and strong
And the flag droops in the rain.
Wrapping its shredded fingers
Round the wretched staff,
Soaked wet; decaying.
The world is savouring your demise
Green-White-Green.
I hear the church bell tolling
And voices chanting sorrowfully
The *Requiem*, fallen emblem.
Who sings the *Nunc dimitis*?
When will your Resurrection come?
Who will sing the *Ressurexit*?

THE CITIZENS PRAY

Master!
Wash our feet
And give us food to feed
Lord of the city of the Rock
Hear our plea.
Keep our roads safe
Keep us safe in our homes
Heal our wounds and
For our ailments, provide hope.
Provide great soldier, for our schools what the . . . .
Shaarrup!
Wretched lots!
Shaarrup!Bloody civilians!

Turn away fast, bloodied country-men
And look up to Him beyond the clouds then.
To the master who alone provides.
To Him who washes all feet.

THE DUNG BEETLE

Why do you roll your ball of dung,
your rear to lead the way?
Why do you hide your face away
From those along your route?
Away from what you choose to do?.
Is it the stench, or perhaps the shame,
Or just a part of the game?
If it is the stench, then stop the trade!
If it is the shame, resign!
Or borrow the cloak of the night,
To save yourself the lash from angry tongues.

CONSCIENCE

Why walk in the night
If you fear the lights
from harmless glow flies?
The harmless call of the owls?
The rustling in the undergrowth?
Why do you shiver,
Covered with goose pimples
At the sound of broken twigs?
The chipping of insects and
The dashing flights of innocents nights bats?
Why do you swing into reflex-like actions
Feverishly drilling fire holes
Into the garment of the night?
Why do you blame the sun
For setting; the dusk for sneaking away?
It was yours all day.
Why blame the moon
For her absence now
When surely you know she has her schedule?
And the stars of the night
For hiding behind the rain clouds mid rainy season?
Achaba the goliath
Why are you whistling in the dark?
The answer is there; gangster
There in your heart.

GOD'S OWN COUNTRY

Fascinating rolling hills.
Captivating mountain ranges.
Those have never in history known
To blow their tops; coughing out larva and smoke.
Throwing up tremendous spittle of liquid fire
In feats of great anger.

Blue, grey and lovely;
Are the heavens above this land.
Those have never in times of sorrow
Flooded these hills and slopes with tears,
Soaking and slicing off the hills
In great torrents of slurry.

Great and gorgeous
Are these two meandering lordly ribbons.
Those in drunken fits, have never habitually
vomited shamefully
Their bowels contents on their flowing garments

Cool and soothing,
These winds blowing
Flowing across the plateaus, and down the mountain slopes
Into the valleys or moving across the vast plains
Winds which never in hurried flights twisted foliage,
Flipped a tent, a thatched roof
Or in total madness jump out of
The gathering clouds hitherto taxiing;
Into a twisting reckless death dance.
Uprooting, crushing, maiming and killing
All in its path.

So caring is our land
That in her painful visceral movements
Twists and rolls not too vigorously
Nor too obtusely
To hurt the baby on her lap
The sleeper in the cot.
Or she in tragic falls!
Cracking some ribs and ruining
her most treasured sets of china!

No freezing or chilling weather
Just enough to call for sweaters
Not a roasting dehydrating clime
But that much to expel in copious sweat
The minor worries; little ailments
of the mind and body.
No night intrusion on the day
But true full nights and sunny days.

And so
No compelling forces of nature
No true challenges to the nation
No blood and sweat situation
No compelling reason to urge forward
This sleeping giant; that claims to be
God's own country.
Hence this nauseating near stagnation
This snail slow intermittent pumping of the heart
Of the giant of Africa.

THE SONG OF THE FESTIVAL CHRONICLER

He emptied our treasury to wine and dine
And much he stacked in foreign lands
Claiming in comfort he does recline
Osetẹbẹlẹ
The name of the greatest leach
That the system ever bread.
What peace he has I do not know.
The peace perhaps
Of the pregnant sluggish clouds
That precede the destructive tornado.
The peace of the latent volcano
Awhile before the crater is re-breached.
And so dear friends, hear me out.
When the gourd of cankerworms got smashed
Fear gripped the trees in the forest land
Their branches in agony trashed
Behold, the fronds of palms in agitation lashed
While the grasses of the plains hugged the ground
In painful strain and fright.
Guilt vacates the head of the red plumed Odidẹrẹ
And lands squarely
On the sacred head of blue plumed aluko
Causing other birds to rise in flocks
Sputtering in greatest disgust.

ANGUISH IN THE MAZE

The owls perch on our roofs
Alternating their calls of doom,
Chilling the blood,
Goose-fleshing the skin.
The dogs bark no more
To scare intruders off
But whimper and whine unnervingly every night
Strangling our sleep.
Okete is out roaming at high noon!
Abomination! Abomination!
Mermaids are seen swimming the entire lengths
Of our mighty arteries
Splashing.
Emptying the river bowels,
Flooding valleys and great fertile plains,
Washing away our treasured crops
Our future.
And jut before our seasonal harvests
Heads of rampaging elephants
Trampled and ate up fields of bumper crops
Casting away the fruits of our labour
In those tremendous bowels of theirs
To excrete in faraway lands
indigestible valued nuts and seeds
Forming new greens, providing new crops
Out of reach of our frail limbs,
Our famished bodies.
And now colonies of trap-wise rodents
Have gnawed numerous holes in
Our neglected stores of past seasons' harvests.
There they live and multiply.
Their grainy faeces fill the punctured sagging sacks
Leaving a stale stench of our destroyed hope
Hanging in the air.

Great Oracle
What do you see in our eyes?
What have you whispered in our ears?
That time is near the redeemer will be here?
That the mermaids will splash no more but
Surface and recline with mirror and comb in their hands?
That a great rat catcher, poison and traps in hand
Like the Pied Piper of Hamelin would appear
To wipe them out or their population thinned?
That the rampaging giants will in
Reserved forests be contained?
Or when here amongst us, in zoos caged
And in circuses trained and maintained?
Great oracle divine again and again
That we be sure that our time in the maze
Will soon terminate
And the appropriate corridor found
To the hidden exit

SONG OF THE WINNOWERS

Winnowing winds! O winnowing winds!
Come down, the distant wooded hills
Come fast across the grassy plains
Rush down on the back of this maturing sun
Down across our threshing ground
To rid these thrashed grains of their unwanted garbs
Fly down helpful winds
And give respite to these lungs,
Rest to these arms, bearing the winnowing trays.

Again and again since this warmth grew right,
We have made our clarions calls
Sang our enchanting invitation songs
For the wind; in vain.
For, the chaffs and the grains entangled
Still dive in common lanes thereby
Ordering these energy sapping encores.

Sorting wind
You have left your tether up on the hills
Without your strength of will
Or perhaps lost in flight, star feathers of your thrusting wings
And so, again and again you sleep walk
Into this labour camp, fiddling with our threshed harvest heaps
crinkling in the sun.
Hearken to our calls, sorting wind
And steel your nerves.
Flap a little harder;
And faster,
For a fruitful descent
Unto this forlorn labour camp.

THE FATHERLAND

When I come back to this world again
Make me a Chaka
The black Napoleon Bonaparte
Expanding my realm, defending my land
Falling if it comes; for,
Dulce et decorum est pro patria mori

Make me a Rommel
The desert fox or
"Monty" the 'stormy petrel';
The great fox catcher
Make me the free-wheeling general Patton
"Old blood and guts'
Or the three rolled into one,
For the love of my land,
My country.
Then let me die; die in action if be, since
Dulce et decorum est pro patria mori

A Nelson will fit me fine.
Or a Dayan—one single peeper each
And ready to loose the other
For the love of their fatherland.
Put me in the hazardous Haganah.
In Tito's elusive fighting force.
Make me a Yoni of an elite squad.
A soldier of the rising sun or
A member of the English Light brigade; one of
The six-hundred who gallantly rode
Into the valley of death.
Drop me alone and at night
Or along with mates
Behind enemy lines
Wrecking, kidnapping,
Harassing, and perhaps dying.
For;
Dulce et decorum est pro patria mori

Duke et decorum est pro patria mori
Sweet and glorious, yes
To die for the fatherland.
But not with these parading mobs
Surely not this time around but
When next I come.
And perhaps if values remain this way
I may ask my God
For a better paternal country
Not this
Where greatness in death does not exist
For men who choose that glorious exit
Not this
Where pips and stripes form the ruling bunch
But brigands rule the day and night.
Not this
Which land flows with milk and honey
But gets drained, into foreign countries.

PASSING EASILY THROUGH

So many times that
I have seen the camel leap through
the needle's eye!
No, not transformed into liquid
And finely jet streamed through the eye
But just as it is
Loopy neck, humpy back,
Sagging sack
On long steely awkwardly positioned props
Dive in one mysterious neat flow
Making a passage through the needle's eye!

In our citadels of learning
In revered chambers of our law courts
In the various Temples of the Lord
In our Assemblies and in the Senate
In our ports and at our borders
On the city streets; the nation's highways
In the stony bowels and wire-laced muscles of our hearts
In every niche of our lives
In this land
The camels are passing through.

WASTED PIPS

From well irrigated desert farms
Around the numerous Kibbutzims
The orchards thrive, rich in fruits
Plump golden Jaffa fruits
Abound in markets, stores and homes.
But never however, in Haifa city
Jerusalem or vibrant Tel
Kibbutz roads or desert routes,
did I see discarded pips
from carelessly disposed fruits.
Old pips are not strewn around
but preserved and reserved
to raise a new crop of trees!.
And so it is in other lands.
Groves and groves of Europe's farms
Hectares un-end on American lands
But never a fruit untimely plucked
With pips smashed or scattered,
As it is in this state of ours.
Pips and pips every where
Except in the barracks their rightful place.

ZIMBABWE ON INDEPENDENCE

Welcome to the fold
Welcome.
You've fought your fight and won
But before the tap-root holds the depth
Before the laterals grip for strength
Learn to shout for help for others
With mouth tightly closed but loud enough
to be heard and deciphered.
Learn to weep for others softly
With eyes tightly closed
Tight enough to send your tears back the other way
Deep into your hearts to steam unseen.
That for now is the way for this game
But if your tears must flow in convention
Let not the torrents blur your vision.
For when we weep, we still see.
Learn sister learn
Learn to growl and bark
And not bark and bite
For after all, in most cases,
With some hard ferocious barking,
The dog achieves its aims.

THE LAUREATE

Oh no!
This disquieting noise again.
What will it be this time
The real Volcano or
The growing time bombs
in the white farm lands?
I will let it ring on perhaps . . .

Stubborn informant
Why don't you keep your peace.
Hello, hello

Hello
My Lord we've hit them again.

Done what again?
Oh no! no! no!
Where again?
Soweto?
Johannesburg?
On their bus?

No, your grace
Our brother has got it

Oh my Lord, my God, damn it!
Damn the white man.
The whole white world!
My brother bought it?
Oh my God!

You are swearing my Lord!
I said our brother in Neegeeria

My brother was in the area?
O Christ my Lord my God.
May your will be done
Which area? Kumalo; where?
Hello, hello.

Not here in Southern Africa your grace
Neegeeria, Neegeerian
No; no;
Yes
The Nobel Prize!
The Nobel Prize!
The Nobel Prize for literature to a Neegeerian

O splendid, splendid
God bless him.
God bless him.
What do you call him?
Shoeyeenkar?
O, truly African name!
Truly African!
You almost killed their peace

No my Lord Bishop, it was the phone.
It stirred up the tumult calming in your heart.
It disturbed the peace that you won
The peace from the chaos.

Right, right you are.
You say a Nigerian scholar won their heart?
Yes my Lord
Most of the English speakers
And the real English white men
Do not understand why
He cannot be understood by the common.
Yet he is not a dreg writer
For, he grew up in their colonial institution.
He trained and practiced among their best too!
Some think the pigment of his English
is as dark or black as his body's.

So the Americans approved it too?

They are baffled by the choice Lord Bishop
They x-rayed and with computer infected minds
Analysed and diagnosed his works
And at the end made an award
with citation laced with hidden barbs
". . . . written in his native vernacular English
of West Africa"

Oh my God, this is apartheid
in English literature!

Yes my lord, the word apartheid is English
And America is England
Only without a Queen or a King!
How to God I pray and wish
That his cash will not be
In the devalued currencies
Of English West Africa.

Yes son; I wish so too.
Just like my award has devalued
To the reigning chaos of South Africa
And its bastardised English.
Did the French comment?

Yes your Grace.
Very French comment I must say.
"He followed the trail of our Leopold
Then blazed further and wider
In the dark continent of higher literature.
Just like our Claud Simon before him
Our own language laureate
Who we do not understand"

Well, well, bless him; bless him
Where else will our pigmentation permit an acceptable transparency?

It appears exhausted for now.
Completely exhausted.
I say not in this century
Not in any of the sciences for now.

Perhaps in the fine art
Should they now decide
To include.

No, no, never my Lord Bishop
Even then, if no superior white
Michelangelo will resurrect
His state and that state within a city
Will make sure he does.
Just as the physicist Ernst Ruska
Whose feat in the twenties
only matured late in the eighties.

Then where do we go
From here
If we know how to go.

No my Lord; where are we now?
That is the question
Not where do we go from here

Exactly.
Exactly.

Good night my Lord Bishop

Good night my son.

THE CURE FOR A THOUSAND ILLS

"Touch and go
Touch and go"
Shouts the itinerant drug man.
"Your toothache gone with a touch
Of touch and go
A huge relief for a tiny sum"
A small crowd gathered to buy the "touch and go"
And another drug that cures a thousand ills.

"Kill and go
Kill and go"
Sang the huge crowd of marching youths
Run for dear lives brave youths
For soon they start to shoot
They hear the order 'go'
but are deaf to calls for 'halt'
The large crowd melts at the crack of guns
Before this cure for a thousand ills.

Come and go
Come and go
The parrot sings its copy-cat song
And so they came and left
Left as they came
The poll box picked; the trigger implants
Leaving no cure for our thousand ills

EVOLUTION

Horribly weird and revolting
These species, that Darwin curiously missed.
These species, perhaps extraterrestrial,
That a short while ago invaded this land Nigeria
Like those terrible water weeds on our lagoons
and coastal rivers.
They know no truth, nor care
for what honour and morals demand.
For since they had left in haste uncleared
And through the back exist of heaven's workshop
When the spirit of truth and honour; loyalty and selfless service
got handed out!
Their consciences—deep and dark ravines and
the planning abode of Satan.
Their bowels—as if with hardest concrete set
While their hearts; wire meshed
Will not a drop of charity and love contain
But run dry straight
Evaporating these virtues like rain
in brief showers, on desert sand mid-day.

As for service to the pleading folks
To wash, dry, and anoint their tired swollen feet
Bind their wounds; ensure they feed
The brutes, which let no crumbs from the high tables fall
Would with barbed palms their feet scrub
and with pepper-laced water wash.
Then while their people in pain writhe,
The looters divert funds for care to foreign lands
With great zest.

Land of the statue of liberty
The Trafalgar square;the Big Ben
Taj Mahal and the Eiffel Tower.
Land of the Apian Way and the Coliseum
Lowlands of the windmills and canal streets
Lands of the majestic peaks of the Alps
Land of the great Niagara tumbling mass
Land of the Rhine, home of the autobahns
Land of the rising sun; the Samurai Knights
Land of the Aborigines and their Kangaroos
Did you all this neglect suffer; this pain submit
Did your leaders this treacherous path tread
To arrive the promise land of good governance?
Did they?

BATTON CHANGE

Listen to the sting-less guns booming.
Booming for the new commander, in coming
The control of our wars; our future he takes.
Farewell to him that some truly hate to contain,
But others love to retain
In line with the confusion in the colour of
His flowing "adire" garb;
Dyed light, with copper sulphate stuff or what.
Some saw blue, and others green; while others still
Read the colour as turquoise.

Droop and descend weary flags of yesterday
Fly in the wind you flags of future breeze.
Reload the guns this time with shells real;
Our enemies and problems on all fronts to hit
And the campaigns left unfinished,
you with vigour review and win.
Then shall your twenty-one booms be heard across the land
North to South; East to West.
Welcome Yar' adua
Welcome Vice Goodluck
May your luck truly hold.

ON THE DISCOVERY OF PETROLEUM CRUDE IN GHANA'S OFFSHORE FIELDS

O Columbus! Land a-hoy! Land a-hoy!
Kufuor; Ghana! Oil a-hoy! Oil a-hoy!
On a great pedestal before, you deservedly stood
When Africa, a place in Ghana many thought.
But down the stinking floor you crashed and laid
Then on all fours you crawled in mire and dirt
Scavenging in towns, and hamlets of our West.
Slaving too in cities of their West.
Brave heart; Land a-hoy! Land a-hoy!

Up in your night are stars of gold.
Down in your land a Coast of Gold
And off this coast, black gold in deep riches hold.
Kufuor; let the flag with the sole black star
on the mid golden strip flutter.
Bring your gifted starlets and stars into the arena
their artistry to display.
In celebration, let loose the Black Meteors on the turf
in turn, and watch their sparkling mesmerizing flight
Beat the drums and let Hi–life bands play
For the black gold currents your shores approach
Unstoppable!
But caveat; caveat Kufuor
Be careful that you do not fall
Into the booby trap like some did before.
Surely, the bruises and sprains of your last night's back slide
As the progress mountain you climbed, remains fresh on your mind.
So caveat Ghana.

You can become what you want to be
A black Korea—The Black Tiger if you please.
You can flourish like the Rising Sun—Japan
Or Formosa, O no! Taiwan O! ROC
You can become Black India and
O yes, you can be our China!
Our own Red China!
You can be whatever you choose to be
But be not like you coast mate to the east
Beyond the coast of the ivory Kings
Where Fou-ta Djallon's tears and sweat, into the sea run deep.
The black-gold rich squanderers and embezzlers to the east
Whose citizens in abject squalor still live
Despite decades of the black gold slush flow.
Flow like the waters of the Niger
And the Benue.

CORRUPTION IN THE BLOOD

Before the watchful eyes of mates gathered to share
Ajointly owned piece of meat
A sharer preferring his teeth
to a knife
Succeeds in biting some off and hide
in the pouch of the cheek.
On protests and request for a mouth assets probe
The piece swiftly slides down the throat
straight into the great hold!
Such childish pranks precursors are perhaps
Of the stealing and rampant plundering
of our various treasuries.
Our common assets.

RELIGION AND SPIRITUALITY

INTERVENTION

A wriggling dehydrating earthworm
Marooned in a caking wetland fringe
Barely hidden under some narrow grass blades
In an abode, swarming with preys.
Then suddenly
The sky is pregnant and the winds still.
A few birds hurry away back to their cozy nests
The first drops fell
Hitting the parched surface in a staccato preamble.
Then the down pour
Welcome savior!

A fragile starving grassland spider
Ambushing on an extensive web
Spurn among the tinder grasses and stems
Straddling the overgrown grassland track;
Is jolted by a cracking roaring sound,
Of a massive fire approaching.
Then, the sound of stampeding hoofs
Of galloping horned animals tearing through the track
Towards the spider on its web.
The massive anthers collecting the spider and the web
Riding to safety!
Welcome savior!

A lonely weary traveler
On a dark starless night
Labouring up a hill on his route
towards a travelers inn
Neared a sudden drop, a precipice.
Then a flash of lightening sharp and revealing
tore the laden sky above!
Welcome savior!

MOULT IN THE FOREST

The moult of a big snake
Shredded with time in this tangled niche
The wearer whose new tights
Perhaps already too tight
And by now about discarded
A change of self, many times repeated
Executed in perfect retreat and abstinence
And yet, imperfect!
A mirror image of those inner moults of mine
With lustre re-born
But fade with the dying pains of their re-birth.

VOLCANO—CHIMNEY AND WINDOW OF HELL

A continuous visceral rumble.
Hell
The pre-historic tenant of earth's womb is belly aching;
bellowing; hissing.
Snorting smoke and ash up the chimney and out
ten thousand meters in the sky.
The latest crater
Hell's closed fenestra is now shattered.
The cracked opened furnace, bubbles giant liquid tongues
Skipping!
Overflowing the lips
Creating rushing cascading flows
Of super-hot magma down the slopes and shoulders
Charring
Cremating
Fossilizing.
But there deep down below
Hell neither chars nor maims
But burns unconsumingly; eternally!
Inflicting pain and agony the book says
On the goats separated from the sheep.

HIDDEN POWER AND STRENGTH

Without a spine
Without a hand
to drive the pile
You bore through the earth so fast
And with great ease that
Has for ages remained a puzzle to man.
In the easiest of terrains
And with all the rains,
Man needs for deep penetration
A driving force to maintain
A passage through the ground
for pegs and piles.
And for some soil a special bit
Or else the earth resists.
What bit cones this flowing weakness?
What stiffens your weak muscled trunk?
For this perfection; this strength

The strength of the weak spider's web
And the caterpillar's silk thread
The magic of night flight in bats
The hidden power of the spineless worm
And that in the core of the minutest dust
The atom,
Must have a source for sure.
Therefore I shall search for that source.
Seek the special bit; the coning power.
I shall weave my own web,
My own fragile web of strength.
Obtain the night vision capability
For my flights and struggles in this darkness,
This treacherous and tempting world.
I shall split and harness the atom
Of the Word.

CLOSING SHOWS

The green forest's velvet showl
Has now exchanged for the colour gold
Autumn's brush has painted all foliage
Yellow, brown, pink and gold
The closing show before the cold
Autumn, has surely spied on summer's sun
The way to end in glorious shades.
The silvery sun of a brilliant day transforming
To a golden orb; plants a goodnight kiss on the cheeks
of the western sky
Leaving coats of gold in various shades.
Of dull and brilliant yellow;
Of red, brown and lovely pink
A beauty of a closing show

A violent persecutor of the nascent church
Then a blinding light on Damascus road
Persecutor to a nurturer transformed
Darkness to light; Saul to Paul!
The spread of the Word
A breakout from the bridge-head city!
A blitz capturing the gentile world
A beauty of a closing show.

THE FESTIVAL DANCE

I can see the fire
Fueled now and again
Logged to last the night till dawn
The dawn of the festival.
I can see my legs among the legs
My feet among the feet
Stamping
Intricately moving
Struggling for possession of a piece
Of the choked dancing space.

I am dancing.
Dancing to the rhythm
The rhythm of the stamping feet
The trashing canes
The praise and scathing songs
And the cracking fire.
I am dancing to the cracking noise of the fire
Yes, the fire that I see and
The darkness that envelops us.

The darkness; the envelope!
No;
Dance not again for this fire, this light
The embers that glow for a while
And dies!
The fire in an envelope of darkness!
Rest my feet, rest.
Rest and prepare for the new dance.
The dance for His son, our Christ
That Son; our Sun
The Light that licks the darkness clean!
Showing the faces of dancers redeemed
And the faces of new watchers too.

PAIN OFFERING

Prolong this pain I pray
This discomfort
And make it last
Just a short while.
Perhaps the night.
This pain,
A microcosm of your pains
Your labour of love
From Gethsemane
To Golgotha.

OMEN

Did the owls in relay call?
And the dogs moan, whimper and whine?
Did the Okete roam in broad day light?
Did the people say
The mermaid passed down the river Niger and the Benue?
Did you hear the witches whistling last night?
Do I hear the folks exclaiming—Opari! Opari!
It is finished!
It is finished!

MY GREGORIAN CHANT
NOTE BOOK

You claim not the clarity of
The archaic type-writer's characters.
Or that of its modern successor the computer.
You never saw the interior of an ancient printing house
With its chattering clanging humming *pre-historic* machines
Or that of its modern cousin the electronic press.
You do not have the adornments of musical notes
Of musical scales, cleffs and rests
All you are
A note book of non-classical hand written pages
Of four scores and six different chants.
Chants with notations personal to the scribbler.

O how much I miss the throb
The heartbeat of the Catholic church.
O how much I thirst for those spirit filling, soul lifting chants
Before my countless trips
To the holy enclaves
The ancient monasteries of Europe *via*
Some three dozen compact discs and tapes.
How much I enjoyed these spiritual odysseys
These five years of the re-discovery.

POST HOLY COMMUNION—YOU ARE A MONSTRANCE, A CIBORIUM

Lift up high this special monstrance
Lift it in the consecrated hands of your soul.
Daily carry it through the people and
Bless all that cross your path.
All who cross the path of your thoughts.
Bless them all
With Him who resides in this central core of your soul
Wield not this monstrance to hurt
Nor discard for the atmosphere to corrupt.
Use not the most high's Ciborium
As garbage can; your trash receptacle.
But as a gift vessel of highest worth
From the celestial court
To hold the greatest, worthiest gift of all!
Bring it back after your daily toils
After each night of rest
Clean.
And if perchance stained,
Scrub and polish until it shines again
Then lift Him up again
And proceed to display.
Daily.

GRATITUDE

With gratitude Lord I
Have come and will come again
To this corner of your house.
I confess and I beseech you
That you wash me clean, and keep me tuned
As I trudge along this rugged path to you.

FIRST ATTENDANCE AT A PENTICOSTAL CHURCH SERVICE

He stands on the pulpit
speaking in tongues
Walks down the aisles
breaking into songs.
Dives again and again
Into the sacred pool of his Holy Spirit
Scooping fresh words, the tongue to sustain.
Words and phrases dozen times repeated.
The abracadabra of the 'born again'
The congregation
Unlike the Pentecost of Peter and company
Went into a frenzy
Shouting their two thousand different supplications
At the same time!

The leader, roaring control interjections
Intermittently calling for prayers.
Then going into a sudden fit of vibration
Arrested sharply with a powerful hiss
Like some angry pre-historic land animal
Or a sea monster, breaking the surface to exhale.
Then the tongue twisting resumed.
But none could hear in his or her language
Like at the Pentecost of Peter and company
It is the preserve of this leader.
The preserve, of our new Apostles.

THE MIRACLES

You stretched your holy hands
Across death's dark barrier
To bring back to life
The daughter of Jairus.
The son of the widow of Naim
And in Bethany, your friend Lazarus.
Author of life,
You raised them all and so I pray
That in your infinite love and mercy
You raise back to life this spiritual carcass
And give peace again to my tortured soul
Songs of praise and worship to these parched lips.

ASSAULTS

When the land slides
Or the dam bursts,
And down rushes the satanic floods,
Be there to save me Lord.
For what power do I possess
To withstand such onslaught
Except your assurance, your word.
Just as you stopped the tempest
In Galilee on the sea
Just as you stopped the flow and
split the red sea
For passage through of your chosen people
Pursued by the massive hoards of
Egyptian enraged warriors.
Stop these frequent rushing horrors
From Satan's trap of water logged
hills and dams of my life.
And move me quickly if they come
Safely to higher grounds.

BEGIN AGAIN

Rise from your fall and walk.
My son, rise from your fall.
Roll onto the shoulder of the road
For you are on a highway
Trafficked by fast massive loads
on hard and biting wheels.
So son; *surge et ambula!*
Arise and walk: be fast
Lest the juggernauts massive wheels,
Or hardened steel chain-wheels
Shred you to minced meat.
Then the steel rollers flatten you
Into the surface of the road,
On this route to the oasis.
So roll over fast!
Surge et ambula!
Stand up and walk on.
Smartly!

SWEET LORD

Your comforting peace dear Lord
More than ever before, I feel.
Covered with wound and slime
You washed and healed.
Bleaching my browned garment white
With your precious flow every time.
You alone know this spineless creature
And hence, in the greatness of your compassion
Forgive these grievous crimes.
Sins of thoughts, words, and deeds.
Preventing their daily sprouting
On this compost heap.
All of me I fully expose
Though your eyes do see intensely
The tiniest niche of my heart; my life.
Help me to do your will
From sunrise to sunrise.
Until you choose to call for
What belongs to you.

HELL IS THERE

None has ever in history claimed to have
In excavation set sight on
Or in deep mining hit or scratched on
What they were sure or perhaps felt
Could be the feared and elusive gate
Of the furnace hell.
Since none has made the journey in quest
And returned the tale to tell
Or the location to give,
Much doubts in some minds still remain.
But He has placed many spouts
(Since we cannot this gate locate)
Perched on hills and mountains high
For all to see and in awe sigh.
Hot smoke and ashes snorted
Ten thousand meters high!
Boiling bubbling pots of magma
Leaping over the lips of the craters
The windows of hell
Cascading down the cheeks
In rivers of death.
A terrifying spectacle for doubters
As well as believers to behold.
Their thoughts to re-set,
For sure, it is there.

TRIBUTE TO Olu'wo AN Orisa of Ọlọrun-Ọba'risa

Olu'wo my lord
You whose mouth takes in
The biggest festival bean-loaf
But widens in vain to permit
The smallest whole Kola-nut.
You who stands on toes
To glimpse into the years beyond
Whose molars are the blade of hoe
Ah!
I leave your praise to those still there
For I have not been brought back to you
In manners prescribed.
But my lord,
I feel qualified even now
To chant these lines of your tributes
Even if just for the fun!
For who answered your calls
When you moved down the mountains,
On your annual visits
Into the valley below?
You would have gone back then my lord
To your cave in the forest beyond,
If after your third call
he did not answer.
I am his seed.
The child from the clan of the healing pot
The child of those whose voices when not heard
No voices are heard.
The child, of the six grinding stones.
Six grinding stones, with holes in their centres
Rendering them unusable for grinding.
I shall learn the rest of your tributes
Learn your songs; your rituals
Learn all about your festival
If only to teach my kids
Their ancient past.

COURAGE

I am lame and blind
and have been left behind.
Lost; on this treacherous terrain.
Hungry, all energy drained.
No water for my thirst to quench
No shade for a rest on this long difficult climb
to your city on the crest.
I glance to the rear
And nothing I could see or hear.
Only darkness and the cry
of the passing birds of doom.
But deep down in my soul
Is this grain of a feeling
Like a tiny perk of light
A distant glow inviting.
In this total darkness,
I feel perhaps a silhouette ahead leading.
And a voice of that feeling saying
"Courage son, courage.
I am your hope; the spring of your heals
The strength of your knees
The power of your eyes
And, the light in your soul.
I am the cleansing flame
Consuming your weaknesses
Curing your deformities.
I am your spring of life; your food.
I am your guide leading you through
This long and treacherous route.
Courage"

OPPORTUNITY

If you did gulp to full with reckless abandon
That intoxicating drink-power
Or climb to the last rung of the ladder
The shoulders and heads of others as steps of the ascent.
If you did relish or rummage in garbage dumps
of flesh and filth.
Or in any other way got derailed
But got humbled,
And the prodigal's return route you trace
Before the last breath you take
Thank you stars for the humbling touch and recall
And hang on to the greatest gift of all.

GOSPEL

Loud lead voices soon geared into vocal competition
at different points on this same street.
Dissolving the initial sober orderliness of the groups
into a mass of frenzy.
Every night
From praise houses and 'holy' rooms everywhere
Shrapnel of doom lace the tired air.
Making our journey through
This already mined and booby trapped times
A blood curdling nightmare.

THE STRUGGLE

Too many bridge heads have I gained
And lost
In this war whose end I cannot see.
So many battles fought and lost
In this fifty-two years of my struggle.
How many more battles to victory or doom?
How many?
So much training
So many drills
So many pep talks from seasoned drill masters
In the days of my youth, in readiness for
These relentless attacks
And those lost battles of my war.
But now I thank you Lord for the lull
The chance for this re-appraisal
Of the years if rout on the battle fields.
The chance to re-group, re-train, re-fit.
The chance to jettison my lukewarmness
And sharpen my alertness.
Drop the hesitations and
Grab the numerous opportunities
Consolidating quickly and
Expanding the new bridge-head
Fighting towards the objective.
I ask you Lord for your guidance
Your Angels to lead me through those
Dangerous and booby trapped battle fields ahead
To watch my often exposed flanks
Strengthen these flanks and
Sharpen my planned probes and advances
From my newly won bridge head.
Developing them into a roaring break-out
And victory.

THY WILL BE DONE

Fiat Voluntas tua
In sickness and in pain
In hardship of all strains.
Up on the peak and
Down in the valley and ravines of life.
On the dangerous slopes and
Across the level plain
Thy will be done.
Through the blinding storms
And biting winds
Through dangerous swamps
The sucking quick-sand.
Through infested waters, and forests of life.
On desert routes; on easy tracks
And when freewheeling in joy
May thy will be done
Fiat voluntas tua

THE WAY FARER

Great Oasis
The large inviting verdant haven
In this dry vast waste land
Across which I must transverse.
I have searched for you, perhaps lukewarmly
Perhaps ill prepared; with no native guards
No compass and no maps.
And so have lost much precious strength
Following you in mirage cloaks
On numerous wrong routes in this dehydrating vastness.
Too many wrecking, blinding sand storms
Have assailed me, blowing me away from you.
Though my journey great hazards plague
In you my hope will stay.
My dream
To you I trudge.
My source of living water
I thirst for your cold refreshing spring.
I hunger for the sweet fruits of the vegetation.
Come then saviour Lord; my Oasis
Hold my hand in yours
And pull me out of any quick-sand.
Lift me on to your stout shoulders to rest my legs
Then let you desert guides
Lead me on to that place of rest.

THE QUAGMIRE

Eternal King
I am trapped!
Sinking deeper and deeper each day
In this morass of my failings.
I look around but no stump for a heave.
A tree to climb
Strong reeds to hold.
Each pressure applied
Sends me down deeper and deeper
And soon would be neck deep and
then over!
But then, in my helplessness
In this surrounding emptiness
I know you are present.
And that your strong arms
Your invisible long hands
Can pull me out
And ferry me to *terra firma*.

LOVE

You made me drop this low
Surely for things you want me see.
You removed me from this peak
Of the mountain range of fame
To this ravine so deep
Surely, to tame.
Providing me a closer and more complete view
Of the fascination that is you.

DOWN IN THE SLURRY PIT

Snow-white my pig
Why do you roll at will
In this stinking slurry
Grunting in ecstatic satisfaction?
Why do you return to roll in glee
Every time, after I made you quit?
And when you leave to go on stroll
It is to the garbage dumps you go
Foraging
Returning again to your stinking mess
To resume this delight with zest.
Whereas I have provided for your use, *Snow-white*,
My pigsty, scrubbed so clean
And with food and water
To eat, drink and roll in
Come then, my *Snow-white*
And stay in my pigsty.
In my care, love, and peace.

MOUNTAIN FIRE

Against the canvas of darkness
A fluid belt of lapping golden tongues
Flaring and fading at many dozen points
Cleaned the distant mountain range.
No smokes seen.
No cracking roaring sound.
No hovering kites or other birds of prey.
An ill-timed feeding extravaganza
A consuming 'beauty' contouring silently
Up or down the sides
Cleaning
Blending
Leaving black in the place of brown.
Golden tongue
Cleansing flame
Come down and fill our hearts and
"Enkindle in us the fire of Thy love"
Burning all our distortions away.

THE NEW SAINTS

How I wish old heaven admits her new tenants
In the old fashioned way
The saintly and the run-of-the mill repentant
My humble self, when I go
Purified and transferred up from purgatory
Would have wished to meet the saints
All of them.
Angels and Patriarchs
Apostles; Labourers of the Vineyard
Martyrs and products of Purgatory
And join in endless worship and praise
To Him the one and only God.

I do not wish O God
To share your abode with those lots
That made our lives some hell on earth.
Who with guns and daggers rob
Rape and kill their prey, then
Shoot the child between the eyes
For daring to spy on their faces!
And when caught; would hold your holy books
Wear the Crucifix or the Rosary and
March to their death singing songs of praise.

Now Lord
This breeding ground my country
This fertile land of crime and wickedness
Will saturate your Holy abode with strange saints
And then when I come
Will shiver to look at the faces of
Your new breed of saints.
No Lord!
Let them go to where they belong
To roast in hell with masters of
Auschwitz, Treblinca, Dachau and the rest

But God, you are God indeed.
And your ways are surely not our ways
Your mercy has no limit
No sin, no stain, too red, black or brown
Too deep
Too heavy
to bleach.
To forgive.

REBUILDING

Since you rebuilt this lovely home
I have dear Lord found out
That as we pray
and as we play
That as we work
and as we walk.
As we talk
and as we call
On our friends at home
And when alone on our own,
We feel your fragrance in the air.
Feel you gracefully touching our troubled hearts
united again.
We feel you Lord
And hear your frequent calls.
See you in verbal love jabs
Lively giggles and non-irritating whispers.
We see you too in these talking eyes!
These sincere smiles
And the quickly aborted angers.
Now can we sincerely declare
Without any hidden fears
Of charge of pretentious claim
Our adopted family motto
Ubi caritas et Amor,
Deus ibi est
Where charity and love is,
God is.

TIMING GOD FOR ANSWERS

He possess not an hour-glass
Or the nurse's minute sand glass
Nor on His wrist like men, a time piece worn
For His schedule to keep; a current job abort
and to the next plea turn.
So, labour not on time and response of heaven
to pleas transmitted.
For Time himself knows when best to descend
Like the gentle mountain wind
into this valley below.
Descend
Like the night dew on the tress and grasses.
Knows when to flow across
Like the seas coastal soothing breeze
On his people on the beaches.
He comes blessings when He comes.
Glides in answers when it is best
for you.
The right time and
"As gentle as silence".

BUTTERFLYING FOR MIRACLES

With torches in our hands and lenses to the eyes
We search.
Through great rubbles as it were;
We search.
In churches and gatherings of miracles everywhere,
Whose calls and beckons fill the air
Screens and pages of the day;
We search.
Whereas the extra ordinaries abound in every sphere
At every turn on our routes.
Open the eyes of your dozing minds
And there before you lie:
The miracle of the daily rehearsal of death, and
Our morning resurection with the sun.
The sun
That yesterday in the West layed dead,
But in the morning rises in the East.
The miracle of the yam and all seeds
in the soil that rot
And then to new plants spring
New crops yield.
The miracle of the flow of air into your bellows
Giving needed draught to
the fire—the embers of life!
Of course the miracle of the pleasure of that spring!
The spring of the water of life
And the lives that from it begin.
The miracle of the secret port of life
Whose narrow constricted gateway into the world,
The eye of the needle is!
Would during birth, to a great portal transform
briefly;
To let the camel neatly through!
This life in miracle is heavily cloaked.
The world in miracle is truly soaked.

Waste not then precious time
In needless miracle hunts
For the weight of your cross
to feather-weight transformed.
But offer all sufferings and needs to Him
And "as gentle as silence", your miracle comes.
If some good for you it will bring.

TO MY COUSINS PAT AND KATE

Two sibling souls, there at Jesus' feet
One Catherine and the other Patrick.
Two souls with me at childhood our foods did share
Night fables learnt.
And with great grand Mama, life was all care.
Three souls separated by death
Death in fire and smoke.
Two spirited; the third left behind.
Left in this world of sin and greed
Unsure of what the end would be.
Since your white no dirt, no stain did touch,
The key to the Sacred Heart for sure you've got.
The ears of the Mum of Mercy to you incline.
So I pray you Pat and Kate my cause to plead
For a happy re-union of our trio.

BOGGED DOWN IN THE MIRE

Clamped in the mud as it were
In the vicious grip of the mire
Close to the dwindling water hole
Stood a fearsome, desperate buffalo
Statue like, but for the head motions and the moo.
They came at first in cautions moves.
But soon all caution to the air
the villainous rogues threw
as its predicament they rightly read.
They came; the pack of hungry hyenas
And ate their prey from sides and rear!
Their powerful teeth into the hide and flesh sank
Tearing,
As if by them freshly killed, or found a carcass.
Biting away this ferocious bull as it stood
Not contesting.
Powerless.
Grimacing at each bite.
Mooing in great agony.

I shivered as to the book of Psalms my mind recourse
For its lines this scene in the documentary performed.
"A herd of bulls surround me
Strong bull of Bashan closing in on me
Their mouths open, like lions roaring at their prey.
Round about me are vicious dogs
Villainous rogues encircling me
Deliver . . . . my life from the powerful grip of the dogs"
O how truly this scene, these past decades
my life portrays.

Bogged down in the deepest morass of life
But still in encirclement harassed
Not yet the strikes.
And so, I like the Psalmist do now plead
That I be rescued from the powerful grip
of this life's mire.
From the jaws of the lion of death
And ferried out of the quagmire,
Or else that buffalo's fate, I will surely share.

A PLEA TO THE MADONNA

Truly empty!
These spiritual wine vessels.
Empty too
Chests of my temporal needs.
Empty
like those receptacles of Cana Galilee
Which by a gentle mother's plea
And His ministry schedule reviewed, got
With vintage stuff refilled.
Perpetual Help; your intercession I hereby plead.
That these empties of mine be refilled
Like trillions since that marriage feast.

RESCUED

Pulled out of this soggy mock
Now make me through the dangerous morass walk.
Not cautiously as the ancient chameleon does
Or gingerly as the big swamp birds
land and tread
feeding.
But in parade marching steps
Hopping;
Striding
And then, goose stepping.
Walk me through this quagmire
That has held me fast in its lips
Up to my waist
Not just for a while,
But for a period the garb of eternity donned.
Inching higher
towards the crown every hour!
Since this journey a desert and the sea I
still will transverse,
Let not my route through some quick-sand pass.
As for the varying moods of the sea
Those roaring crashing watery hillocks do appease.
Smoothing their brows with gentle caressing breeze.

ADAM AND THE GARDENS

In the garden paradise of pleasure
Beneath the fruit tree of good and evil
With a *caveat* not to touch
But into its consumption I was lured
And so I fell
I Adam, fell.

On a sorrow drenched night
Across the brook of Cedron on the Mount of Olives
Under a tree
On His knees a heart in great agony boiled
Overflowed
Soaking the soil in sweat drops of blood
His will surrenderiing to His will
As the cup he began to sip
And so to my rescue came
The second Adam to the fight.

The olive tree of sorrow
Transfered its abundant life giving fruits
To the tree on the place of the skull
Smeared; patch-soaked with blood!
Come;
Come
To this tree for food and rest
All you that hunger and with thirst
No *caveat* on the trunk attached
No;
None.

GLOSSARY

LIFE AND DEATH

Poem 5. *LBW*—A foul in the game of cricket.—Leg before wicket

Poem 8. (a) *"Take not the millipede . . . ."* Yoruba advice to the dead to abide by the rules in heaven; discarding completely all things earthly. Things represented by the earthworm and the millipede which are detestable. (b)*" Requiescat in pace"*—Rest in peace.

Poem 22. *Oluwo*—The deity worshiped by the people of Ogidi in Ijumu land.

Poem 27. *Calliope and Erato*—Greek muses—Two of the daughters of Zeus the Greek god of the sky.

Poem 28. *Phoebus*—Greek mythology—Apollo the god of the Sun

Poem 35 *Abiku*—A child believed to have been born into this world before, died, and was born again of the same mother. A re-incarnated child.

Poem 36. (a) *"Chant of Gregory"*—*Gregorian Chant*—The liturgical Latin music of the Catholic Church. (b) *Erato*—Greek Muse. One of the daughters of Zeus the Greek god of the sky, and ruler of the Olympian gods.

Poem 37. (a) *Armatto*—A Ghanaian poet who died in a car crash. (b) Te Deum laudamus—A Latin chant of thanksgiving to the Holy Trinity.

Poem 40. (a) *Abuja*—Nigeria's new capital city. (b) *Suleja*—A city formally known as Abuja but surrendered its name to the newly created Nigerian capital city.

Poem 41. *Okete*—A large nocturnal rat which when sighted during the day is regarded as a bad omen.

Poem 42. *"Deo volente"*—God willing.

Poem 45. *El-Shaddai*—One of the Judaic names of God.

Poem 49. (a) *Buka*—Local eatery. (b) *Kia kia pronto*—A slang combination of Yoruba and Spanish words meaning—instantly or without delay.

Poem 52. (a) *Victor Ludorum*—Latin—Winner of the games. (b) *Clio*—The Muse of History. (c) *Calliope*—The Muse of epic poetry. (d) *Erato*—The Muse of love and erotic poetry.

Poem 56. "*Deo gratias*—Thanks be to God.

Poem 57. "*Requiescat in pace*"—Rest in peace.

WAR AND PEACE

Poem 1. ". . . . the forces at the Horn" The forces fighting at the Horn of Africa.

Poem 2. *Tapa*—Nupe tribe of today's Niger State of Nigeria.

NATURE, COUNTRY LIFE AND SEASONS

Poem 1. *Alago*—Watch repairer. (b) *Alekesondar*—Alexander.

Poem 5. (a) *Hercules*—A bicycle brand preferred by the village farmers then for the ruggedness. (b) *Rudge and Raleigh* other more elegant brands of bicycle.

Poem 12. "*until matins*"—Matins—2am prayer time by Monks in the Monastery. Matins ends at dawn

Poem 20. (a) "*et al*"—and others. (b) "*et cetera*"—and so forth.

Poem 25. *Awulele*—(Okun-Yoruba dialect) meaning Ululation.

Poem 31. "*FESTAC 77*"—Festival of Arts and Culture of Africa and Blacks in Diaspora held in Lagos Nigeria in the year 1977.

LOVE AND PASSION

Poem 2. *Victor Ludorum*—Winner of the games.

Poem 4. *Zeus*—The Greek god of the sky and head of the Olympian gods.

Poem 6. (a) *Foliorum Silbula*—An eighteen century poetry collection of British, Greek and Latin or Italian poets. (b) "*et cetera*"—"and other things."

Poem 9. "*Alea iacta est*"—The die has been cast.

Poem 20. *Medea*—A colchian woman in Greek mythology. The daughter of the king of Colchis, and wife of the hero Jason. An enchantress and sorceress, she helped Jason collect the Golden Fleece.

Poem 23. (a) *Cleopatra*—Beautiful queen and last Pharaoh of Egypt—69-30BC. Had affairs with Augustus Caesar. (b) *Nefertiti*—Great wife of the Egyptian Pharaoh—C. 1370BC-C.1330BC.

POLITICS

Poem 1. (a) *The Requiem*—Prayer chant for the dead in the Catholic Church. (b) *Nunc dimitis*—Chant of praise (c) *Ressurexit*—Chant of Resurrection at Easter.

Poem 7. *Okete*—Giant nocturnal rat found in parts of West Africa and seen in the day time only when escaping threat.

Poem 9. *"Dulce et decorum est pro patria mori"*—Latin proverb—It is sweet and glorious to die for the fatherland

Poem 11. *"pip"*—The seed in an orange. Also the rank insignia on the shoulders of military or other uniformed disciplines.

Poem 16. *"adire"*—Yoruba name for "Tie and dye fabric."

Poem 17. (a) *Kufuor*—John Kufuor, President of Ghana (2001-2009) (b) *Caveat*—Careful—a warning enjoining one from certain acts or practices.

RELIGION AND SPIRITUALITY

Poem 8. *Opari*—Yoruba for—It is finished.

Poem 10. (a) *Ciborium*—Large metal receptacle for holding consecrated Host prior to distribution to the communicants. (b) *Monstrance* also known as *Ostensorium* is the vessel used in the Catholic Church and the Anglican Church to display the Consecrated Host.

Poem 15. "*Surge et ambula*" (Latin)—Get up and walk.

Poem 18. (a) *Orisa*—A lesser god. (b) *Oba'risa*—The supreme God.

Poem 23. *"Fiat voluntas tua"*—Latin—Thy will be done.

Poem 25. *"terra firma"*—"solid earth" or "firm ground"

Poem 29. (a) *Treblinka*—German Nazi extermination camp in Germany—World War 2. (b) *Dachau*—The first of the Nazi concentration camps opened in Germany—WW2. (c) *Auschwitz*—A network or complex of concentration and extermination camps operated by the Third Reich in Poland WW2.

Poem 30. *"Ubi caritas et amor,Deus ibi est."*—Where there is charity and love, God is.